Courageous Faith-Bold Witness:

A History of The South Dakota
District of the Lutheran Church - Missouri Synod

Howard Koosman

ISBN: 1-57579-325-3

Library of Congress Control Number: 2005911282

Printed in the United States of America

PINE HILL PRESS
4000 West 57th Street
Sioux Falls, SD 57106

Dedication

Dedicated to the glory of God
-- Father, Son, and Holy Spirit –
with thanksgiving for His grace
reflected in the lives of the faithful saints
who have gone before.

Acknowledgements

Writing a book with this much history for the number of congregations in our District takes the work of a lot of people. The author gratefully acknowledges with thanks the many pastors, teachers and lay people of our District who shared information about their congregation for inclusion in this book. Thanks also to our publisher, Pine Hills Press of Sioux Falls for its guidance and direction in making this project a reality. A special thanks goes to the District Staff – all of whom assisted in various ways in making the task much easier for the author. Special thanks to President Schindler for his support, encouragement and wise counsel throughout the project.

Most sincere thanks goes to Mrs. Julie Pike, the Executive Assistant at the District Office who did all the typing, re-typing and re-typing of the manuscript to get it to its final completion stage for the printer. Her counsel and advice have been invaluable to me in so many ways throughout the entire project. It was indeed a privilege to work with her once again, having worked with her for many years when I was working full-time at the District Office and she served as my secretary and assistant.

Thanks also to Nancy Henrichsen who read and re-read the manuscript finding details that needed additional attention.

Most importantly, I give thanks and praise to my gracious heavenly Father for granting me health and strength throughout the project so that I could see it to completion. His mercies have been new each morning and His faithfulness has never failed!

May this history of our beloved South Dakota District of The Lutheran Church – Missouri Synod be a valuable resource to congregations and our entire District in the years which lie ahead. May it impress upon all of us the greatness and love of our God as He blesses His church when it faithfully proclaims His word to a lost and dying world! May we, today, prove faithful to Him as did our early ancestors.

Howard E. Koosman
Soli Deo Gloria

Table of Contents

Chapter 8 - 1890's - 1900's

Chapter 9 - 1900-1920

Chapter 10 - 1920-1930

Chapter 11 - 1930-1950

Chapter 12 - The Last 55 Years

Chapter 13 - Former Ministries of the South Dakota District

Foreword

The book you hold in your hands is dedicated to the glory of the Triune God – Father, Son, and Holy Spirit. Its pages contain a history of the South Dakota District of The Lutheran Church – Missouri Synod and bear witness to the Lord's abundant blessings.

It took a *Courageous Faith – Bold Witness* to establish the congregations and ministries that make up this District of our beloved Synod. It took a Courageous Faith – Bold Witness to maintain those same congregations and ministries in the face of many challenges. Yet, these pages reflect God's faithfulness. They tell of the Word proclaimed and the sacraments faithfully administered. They tell stories of people and congregations. They help us recall the faith of people who were nourished in Word and Sacrament and thus of God's gifts of forgiveness of sins, life and salvation.

It is my prayer, as you read how God used the men and women who have gone before us, that their example – by God's grace – would prompt you to have and make a Courageous Faith – Bold Witness today. For this book is not simply a history but HIS STORY. Thus may you with the same *Courageous Faith – Bold Witness* pass it on to your children and your children's children and they to theirs. May you with the same *Courageous Faith – Bold Witness* also share that faith in your community and in our world.

We must not forget the past nor miss the opportunities that God places before us in this place we call South Dakota. To God Triune alone, through Christ Jesus, be all glory now and forever. Amen.

Reverend Dr. Vernon L. Schindler, President
The South Dakota District of The Lutheran Church – Missouri Synod

+ October 14, 2005 +

Introduction

To begin the monumental task of recording the history of the first 100 years of the South Dakota District of the Lutheran Church Missouri-Synod is indeed a humbling experience. Even though it takes many, many hours to go through the various histories of the congregations of our District – those that are still operating as well as those that have closed their doors – it's relatively easy to do so. But as one does this, it is nothing short of breathtaking to observe the hand of almighty God and the number of lives that were touched through these ministries.

When one thinks back to the beginning of our beloved South Dakota District just after the turn of the last century, life was markedly different than it is today. Winters and summers on the prairie were extremely difficult. Travel was limited by how much the body could endure because it was often done on foot, horseback or horse and buggy in the summer and horse and sleigh in the winter. Cell phones were non-existent, and seeing friends and neighbors was left for a Sunday at church. The struggles that our forefathers endured in order that the church might grow and be a force in the world are indeed nothing short of spectacular! God's guiding hand was certainly seen repeatedly in the lives of these Christian people who were determined to not only have the Gospel for themselves and their children but for their neighbors and all those who would follow after.

Building of churches and Christian day schools was often done with very meager funds and a lot of hard work from those who felt the importance of the saving Gospel in their lives. And so the church was not only a unit which functioned together on Sunday morning, but did so often during the week as they came together to build, to be edified, to visit, to share and to help carry each other's burdens.

The information that we now share in this book comes from the histories of congregations that we have on file in the archives of our District, from old Lutheran Witness articles as well as stories that were given to us by the good people of our District, including our pastors and teachers who have been an immense help in sharing information about the work of God in their congregation in earlier years. So we say thank you to all those who in any way helped in gathering information that we might leave this book for posterity. It clearly shows God's almighty hand working in the lives of His people in our midst.

Mr. Howard E. Koosman, Archivist
The South Dakota District of The Lutheran Church – Missouri Synod

Chapter 1
Beginning of Missions in the Dakota Territory

"When a number of Lutherans moved into the Dakota Territory in 1874, Reverend Stephan Keyl, missionary to immigrants in New York, notified Reverend J.F. Buenger, President of the Western District. Reverend Buenger asked Reverend C.W. Baumhoefener of Scribner, NE, 125 miles south of Yankton to explore southeastern Dakota Territory with a view toward beginning a new mission field. Thus in 1874 Reverend Baumhoefener started on the trip to Yankton by team. In two days of traveling, only 35 miles were covered. The pastor's ponies were exhausted, since there were no roads and the land was soaked from recent rains. After resting his team for a day, Reverend Baumhoefener returned home.

"Three weeks later he tried to reach Yankton; again he failed. He now reported to Reverend Buenger that it was impossible to reach Yankton by team, the only alternative being to travel by train by way of Omaha and Sioux City. President Buenger then sent Reverend Baumhoefener fifty dollars for traveling expenses.

"Finally arriving at Yankton, Pastor Baumhoefener started his mission work in southeastern Yankton County and was successful in gathering a number of Lutherans at Yankton and at Worms (about 10 miles northwest of Yankton). He urged the people to establish the preaching of the Gospel in their midst and promised to help them in getting a Lutheran pastor.

"When Reverend Baumhoefener decided to return home, he reached Sioux City, IA, before discovering that he did not have enough money to finish his trip home. Being a total stranger in Sioux City and not wishing to impose upon Reverend Buenger any further, he wrote to Dr. C.F.W. Walther of St. Louis about his predicament. Dr. Walther was deeply touched and sent $25 by wire to Reverend Baumhoefener, thus enabling him to reach home. This money was a gift from Dr. Walther's own funds and he refused to accept repayment.

"Reverend Baumhoefener now pleaded with Reverend J.F. Doescher of Fort Dodge, IA, to try to take care of the spiritual needs of the people in the Yankton area. Reverend Doescher responded immediately, and after two trips to Yankton and Worms he settled at Yankton.

"A small congregation was gathered at Yankton at a later date, and an effort was made to establish a Christian Day School at Worms. Candidate Theodore Stiemke, who later became President of the Texas District, was placed in charge of the school. Although every effort was made to make this school a growing proposition, it had to be discontinued because of lack of interest.

"In the years 1875 to 1877 Reverend Doescher was missionary at large in 8 counties: Union, Lincoln, Minnehaha, Turner, Yankton, Hutchinson, Bon Homme and Douglas. The extensive territory and lack of records precludes naming all the places where work was carried on. No fewer than 20 preaching places, however, were served.

"It was in 1875 that Reverend Doescher held a service at the home of Hans George Huber at Heilbronn. The settlers in this area had held reading services even before Reverend Doescher came, and continued with this form of worship when it was impossible for the pastor to be present.

"In 1876 Trinity Lutheran Church at Heilbronn was organized. Twenty-one charter members adopted and signed the constitution. When Reverend Doescher accepted a call in 1877 to become our Synod's first missionary to the Negroes in the southern states, Reverend G.E. Freidrich became his successor. At first Reverend Freidrich served the same 8 counties, but in 1878 he limited his work to central Hutchinson County. The rest of this county was served by Reverend F.E. Melcher, who entered upon the work in 1878. There were no organized congregations or permanent Christian day schools besides those at Heilbronn in Hutchinson County, although temporary schools had been established at three places for shorter or longer periods to provide Christian training for the children of the scattered settlers.

"Reverend Freidrich did not remain in Dakota Territory long. In 1879 he accepted a call as missionary among the Negroes in New Orleans. He contracted yellow fever after arriving there and died shortly thereafter.

"In spite of the great shortage of ministerial candidates at the time (as now) the Mission Board of the Northwestern District resolved to place two candidates in the southern field of Dakota Territory. Reverend J.J. Bernthal and Reverend Andreas Mueller, two candidates, arrived in this field in 1882. The former accepted a call to Scotland. From there he also served Tyndall, and later also Flensburg and Delmont in Douglas County. The latter, Reverend Mueller, served as missionary at large, his field including the counties from Union to Davidson, as far as the city of Mitchell. It was in this year 1882, that St. Paul's (Freeman) was organized."

(Taken from 8.27.57 Lutheran Witness – SD District edition.)

Chapter 2

History of the South Dakota District in Commemoration of its 25th Anniversary

"At the request of President F.W. Leyhe, to write a history of the South Dakota District in commemoration of its 25th anniversary, I will try to do so. As many of the readers of the Church News have not read the 'brief history of the South Dakota District' contained in the pamphlet: '400th anniversary of the Augsburg Confession', I deem it helpful here to reprint the same as an introduction.

"When in the year 1847 the Lutheran Synod of Missouri, Ohio and Other States was organized in Chicago, IL, surely not one of the signers imagined that under 'Other States' the state of South Dakota would be found at sometime in the future; indeed, at that time there was no South Dakota; what is now South Dakota was then part of Dakota Territory, a land where Indians and buffaloes roamed unmolested. But in the course of time white people pushed westward. After overrunning the states of Minnesota, Iowa and Nebraska, the settlers soon entered Dakota Territory. Among these settlers were also many Lutheran families not only of Scandinavian, but also of German descent. While the northern part of Dakota Territory was settled mostly by Lutherans from Germany, the southern part saw many German Lutherans from Russia. These Lutheran settlers were mostly farmers, while other nationalities lived in the towns and cities as businessmen. Therefore we find most of the Lutheran churches on the prairies or in small towns. These Lutherans were not long scattered upon the prairies as sheep that had no shepherd, for the church soon sent its missionaries after these settlers to gather them into organized congregations.

"One of the first missionaries in Dakota was Reverend Fredrich Pfotenhauer, who graduated in 1880. He was sent as traveling missionary for Dakota and Montana and was stationed at Odessa, MN. Others soon followed him, and in 1884 we find the following missionaries in Dakota: Reverend C. Cloeter in Beadle County, Reverend F. Schriefer in Douglas County, Reverend T. Hinck in Grant County, Reverend Charles Otto in Lake County, Reverend A.E. Starck in Minnehaha County, Reverend E. Melcher in Hutchinson County, Reverend A. Mueller in Turner County, Reverend G. Rumsch in Yankton County, Reverend C.C. Metz in Groton, Reverend A.H. Kuntz in White Lake, and Reverend F. Eichhoff in Scotland.

"These missionaries formed a net that would stretch from the northern to the southern part of the state. And this net was drawn westward year after year. These faithful soldiers of the cross followed the settlers wherever they went to feed them with the Bread of Life. Wherever possible they started a mission station, preaching the Gospel, administering the Sacraments and instructing the children in the Word of God. For some time the Missouri River blocked the westward movement, but this obstacle was soon overcome. At the end of the 19th century there was a great influx of settlers. In 1900 South Dakota had about 400,000 inhabitants and in 1903 that had increased to 450,000. The Milwaukee and Northwestern Railroads had built their lines to the coast. Again many Lutherans were among the new settlers, let us here give due credit to Reverend F.C. Gade, who volunteered as a circuit missionary to explore the entire western part of the state. His canvas was very successful, and when in 1907, Reverend T. Kissling was called as missionary to this territory, he in a few months organized 14 congregations, nine of which declared their intentions to become voting members of our Synod. Lest we forget: All these trips were not made by automobile (even a Ford was an unknown thing at that time), but on horseback or with horse and buggy.

"In the year 1905 the Delegate Synod at Detroit, Michigan decided that the Minnesota and Dakota District be divided into three districts. South Dakota now formed a district of its own. This event took place at Freeman in 1906. The first sessions were held June 20-26 of that year. The organization was effected under the supervision of Vice-President Reverend H. Succop of Chicago. Also the President of the Minnesota District, Reverend F. Pfotenhauer was present and assisted us with word and deed. At that time the District consisted of 24 voting and 15 advisory pastors, 26 voting congregations and three parochial-school teachers. The following officers were elected: Reverend A. Breihan of Canistota, President; Reverend J.D. Ehlen of Scotland 1st Vice-President; Reverend F. Oberheu of Wentworth 2nd Vice-President; Reverend C. Rudolph, Secretary and Mr. M.F. Kuehnert, Treasurer. The District was divided into four visitation circuits: the Northeastern (Reverend R. Zimmermann, Visitor), the Northwestern (Reverend M. Pollack, Visitor), the Southeastern (Reverend G. Doege), and the Southwestern (Reverend J.D. Ehlen). In 1912 a new visitation circuit was formed, the Western, beyond the river with Reverend F.W. Leyhe as visitor.

The South Dakota District Convention, 1906

"To the glory of God and to the credit of our District it may be said that the South Dakota District was self-supporting from the beginning; we never asked and we never received any subsidy from Synod. On the contrary, we contributed a good share for the maintenance and extension of other, weaker districts. In 1907 the District's total budget was $6,670.46. In 1929 it had reached the sum of $34,929.33 for budget and $2,297.64 for non-budget purposes. The District now consists of 67 pastors, 85 voting congregations, 23 non-voting and 34 mission stations. The membership now is: baptized 17,452; communicant 10,550; voting members 2,966; 14 day-schools with 303 pupils; ten male and five lady teachers.

"We cannot very well write the history of the South Dakota District without mentioning the name of Reverend J.D. Ehlen. On the 23rd and 24th of March, 1890, he was installed as pastor of Scotland, Tripp and Tyndall, by Reverend M. Waechter. Although he was not the very first pastor in the District he at least remained the longest in it and has done much to develop it. From 1906 to 1912 he was 1st Vice-President and from 1912 to 1918 he was President of the District.

"The language used in doing mission work was predominantly German. How much English was used can perhaps never be ascertained. The first English service recorded was held at the church dedication at Howard in the evening service. Reverend A.H. Kuntz was the speaker. At the present time more English than German is used in the work of our District.

"Every local congregation now yearly celebrates a mission festival. The first mission festival on record in the District is that celebrated at the congregation at Yankton in 1884. The collection amounted to $55.76. a sum unheard of in those days.

"The first two church dedications in the District: Reverend T. Hinck dedicated a church in Faulk county on the 24th Sunday after Trinity 1885. On the second Sunday in Advent 1885, the Wolf Creek congregation in Hutchinson County dedicated its new church."

(Taken from "Lutheran Church News South Dakota District, Missouri Synod September 1931. Believed to have been written by Editor, the Reverend F. Wessler)

Chapter 3

Overview of the LCMS Coming
to the Dakota Territory

When one reads the history of the South Dakota District of the Lutheran Church – Missouri Synod, especially at the time of the settlers, one realizes just what kind of "infinite variety" the state does offer! These early settlers and pastors had to endure many hardships in bringing the Gospel of Jesus Christ to the Lutheran people in South Dakota.

There was a time when there was a Northern District. In 1874 it was divided, with one portion being called the Northwest District which included Wisconsin, Minnesota and Dakota Territory. It lasted only six years and was divided into what was known as the Wisconsin District formed in 1881 and the Minnesota and Dakota Territory in 1882. This new Minnesota-Dakota Territory included areas as far away as Montana and Northwest Canada. Emil Christenson was the first Lutheran minister to serve in the Dakota Territory. He was a graduate of Concordia Seminary, St. Louis, but was not a member of the Missouri Synod. His work was done in the areas of Lincoln, Moody, Minnehaha and Brookings counties.

In the 1870's, many settlers moved into Dakota Territory from southern Russia. The Reiseprediger (traveling missionary) had to find and serve these people. The area northward from Yankton into Hutchinson County was a fertile field for Lutheranism. It was not by accident that the first congregation of our District was started at Heilbronn, just southwest of Freeman.

In 1874 Reverend John F. Doescher was commissioned to serve in Dakota Territory. He reported in 1875 that he was serving 26 stations in eight different counties. It was under Reverend Doescher's direction and leadership that the Evangelical Trinity Congregation Unaltered Augsburg Confession was organized in 1876 at Heilbronn, Dakota Territory. This was the first congregation on record of what became known as the South Dakota District of the Lutheran Church – Missouri Synod. Pastor Dewald was called to serve Trinity Heilbronn, becoming its last resident pastor. The Heilbronn church no longer stands at Heilbronn, but was moved to Hurley where it is still used today by Zion, LCMS members.

Because of the tremendous load for Pastor Doescher and because of health concerns, he was given help in the person of G.E. Friedrich. Candidates Andrew Mueller, C.J. Bernthal and C. Melcher were installed as traveling preachers in the next few years.

Then attention was given to the northern counties of the future South Dakota, when on November 7, 1880 Candidate Friedrich Pfotenhauer was installed to serve Lac Qui Parle County in Minnesota and Grant County in South Dakota including the towns of Milbank, Wilmot and Corona. He organized congregations at Albee (near Milbank) as well as James in Brown County.

Other pastors serving at this time were Reverend P. Rolf, missionaries P. Rumsch and Reverend G. Stark. Reverend Rumsch had five stations at Yankton and Reverend Stark served seven stations in and around Sioux Falls. In 1898 a traveling missionary was sent to work from Milbank and Sisseton to Aberdeen. At the turn of the century, Missouri Synod Lutherans had made such progress in South Dakota that they were looking for autonomy in Synod.

"By now the frontiers had passed far west beyond the larger settlements near Iowa and Minnesota. There was still pioneer work to be done in the church when part of the Lower Brule Indian Reservation was open for settlers as well as other parts of the territory stretching from Mitchell to Rapid City. In 1902 this great field was divided into two sections served by Pastors F. Albrecht and R. Runge.

"Various efforts were made from early times to establish our church in the west river country, including the Black Hills. Among the first efforts to serve this west country was that of Missionary F. Kiess, who worked in the Mansfield, Lebanon, Ipswich area from 1892 to 1897. Kiess writes, 'Making a missionary trip to the Black Hills in 1892, I made the trip with my team and buggy. South Dakota was then a bone-dry state, but not the Black Hills. Saloons were the only place where men and women gathered to spend the time. Usually the largest building in town was the saloon. So we went to the saloon to gather information and meet people. The bartender was a congenial fellow inviting us to board with him, which we did. On Saturday he invited all the people he met to the service to be held the following Sunday. When the day came, men and women arrived early. Being the only meeting place in town, the room was soon packed with all sorts of people from the hills. Sermons were delivered in English and German.' Reverend Kiess stated that a congregation was then formed, although we have no record of how long it lasted.

"In 1903, Reverend F. Gade was installed at White Lake to serve this area. He could serve with a free hand. I will take a few notes from what he had written. 'I hitched up my ponies, took water, some bread and kuchen along, and all rosy with hope for the courageous adventure, I happily toyed with the possibility of organizing a small congregation. In place of roses, however, hopes were often adorned with thorns. However, I met

some Lutherans who told me there was a Lutheran mother south of Okaton who wanted her children baptized. Naturally I sought them out. This was on Wednesday and I was now 127 miles from my home station where I had to hold Divine Service next Sunday.' Can you imagine traveling all those miles with a tired team of ponies in such a short time?"

Because the District was seeking self-government from the Synod it held its first convention at Freeman on June 20-26, 1906. It was in 1928 when the proceedings of the South Dakota District were first printed in English. Soon after the organization of the District also came the organization of circuits.

The first convention of The South Dakota District - LCMS held in Freeman, SD (June 20, 1906)

It wasn't long before congregations were started in Tyndall, Dimock, and Delmont.

A hardship that affected many congregations as well as pastors was at a time when the use of the German language was forbidden during World War I. From some of the history of the Immanuel, Dimock parish, it is recorded that Reverend Hempel, born in Germany, was interned in Utah all during

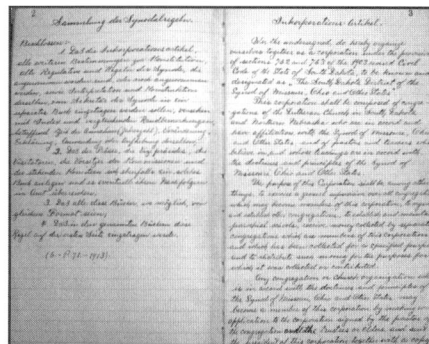

The original Articles of Incorporation for the South Dakota District

the war because of unduly championing the German cause. Many of these German-speaking people who understood very little English, received very little from the English sermons which had to be preached.

And so we see how, even through hardship, God's hand was there guiding and leading His people in our beloved South Dakota District! All praise, honor and glory be to Him!

Chapter 4
Early Congregations 1875-1880

The First Congregation – Trinity Lutheran, Heilbronn, South Dakota
    Among the many immigrants from Europe were some families from the Crimean Peninsula on the Black Sea in southern Russia of German nationality who came to Dakota Territory when it was open for immigrants. Families with names such as Huber and Guenthner came to the Yankton area and traveled some 30 miles north and claimed homesteads in the territory which they later called Heilbronn after the name of their home village in Russia. In 1875, other families from Heilbronn village followed them, namely, Ellwein, Hafner, Walz, Kind, Bauer, and Hein. Joining them from other villages in Russia were families such as Nuss, Pfeiffer, Dewald, Dubs, Haar, Mettler, and Tabert. Some of these settled also in the Wolf Creek region.

    As mentioned in the previous chapter, the traveling missionary by the name of Reverend John F. Doescher, who was stationed at Yankton, came and preached to these people in the Heilbronn community. Preaching had to be done in a home. Often when Pastor Doescher could not be there, the lay people would read from a Sermon Book. Thus the word was preached and taught among them. Records indicate that the congregation called "Die Ev. Lut. Dreienigkeitsgemeinde U.A.C." was organized in 1876 with 21 members subscribing to the constitution. In 1877 Pastor Doescher was called away to serve in Negro missions in southern states.

    The congregation then extended a call to Candidate C.F. Friedrich from New York who accepted and came in 1877. The matter of building a church was most urgent since up until this time worship had to be done in private homes. Living in great poverty in sod houses, oftentimes these early Lutherans sacrificed greatly in order to construct a building. Bricks from Yankton (some 35 miles away) were hauled with horses and oxen in order to build a center for the worship of their God. The congregation also erected a parsonage as well as a three-room building for a parochial school since Christian education of the young was of utmost importance to these early Lutheran Christians. This was the first Lutheran church in the county as well as the first Lutheran Church – Missouri Synod congregation in South Dakota. In 1878 Pastor Friedrich accepted a call away.

Pastor F.E. Melcher of Ohio was then called to serve the Trinity Lutheran Church of Heilbronn. During his ministry at Heilbronn he was married to a girl from the state of Iowa. He was conducting regular services at Heilbronn as well as Menno, Ulmer, Quast, Freeman and Wolf Creek. Horse and buggy meant many days of travel in preaching at the various stations. St. Paul congregation of Freeman was then organized in 1882. In 1888 the parsonage was moved from Heilbronn to Freeman. God's blessing was very evident to Pastor Melcher's ministry when, according to the records, 147 children had been baptized, 149 confirmed, 23 marriages had been performed as well as 31 burials. So Trinity congregation was well established with members increasing in knowledge and growing in Christian faith!

In 1889 Pastor Albert Brauer was called to serve Trinity congregation. Pastor Brauer served longer than any of the pastors who served at Heilbronn - serving there 15 years. It was during his time that the first church burned down and the second church was built as well as the establishment of a parochial school.

What a severe blow to this young congregation when, on a Tuesday night of September 1889, just after midnight, the people discovered that their beautiful brick building was on fire. It was completely destroyed. This was a diabolical act of arson, tempting the congregation to consider whether she would continue to worship her Lord and God. But God had plans for this congregation and, immediately following the burning down of the first church the congregation decided to build a new church. It was erected one mile north of the old church on Henry Hafner's land. This building was in service for 34 years when it became too small and was sold to Mr. Fred Huber. It is still standing on his farm yard, close to the area where it once stood.

Trinity Lutheran Church, Heilbronn- parsonage, church and parochial school

One of the great spiritual blessings which the early history shows that they prized was the establishment of a parochial school where children were brought up to know their Lord and Savior and to live for Him and to serve Him in His Kingdom. Martin Luther's small catechism was taught as well as Bible History each day. In 1893 the congregation called Mr. Jacob Wenzlaff of Yankton as teacher. In 1912 the congregation erected a new school building on the east side of the church. The congregation maintained its Christian school until 1943. When it didn't have enough children to continue, the congregation closed the Christian Day School which had served them for 50 years.

In 75 years of her existence, Trinity had the service of 12 called ministers of Christ and two teachers. The congregation was also very active in recruiting young men from the congregation and especially the parochial school to study for the Office of the Holy Ministry as well as the office of Lutheran School Teacher.

Peace Lutheran Church, Alcester, South Dakota

It was the year of 1875 when a number of German Lutherans who had come from the state of Iowa found themselves without any Lutheran church services. They sought help from the Iowa Mission Board and were served by Reverend Loren Kraemer of Fort Dodge who conducted worship services at Alcester.

Peace Lutheran Church was permanently organized in 1878. Services at first were held every four weeks in various homes which were sod shanties or dugouts. When the Ludwig school was built, it was used for worship services until 1890. In 1890 the first church was erected southwest of Alcester on land donated by Peter Numsen. A parsonage was built in 1893. Reverend Mueller of Marion Junction was serving the new congregation.

It was in 1893 that the congregation called its first resident Pastor, Candidate Christian Wieting. When Reverend Wieting accepted a call to Delmont in 1902, Reverend August Rehwaldt was called. Several pastors followed Pastor Rehwaldt and in 1936 Reverend E.C. Beyer arrived. A number of changes occurred: the seating arrangement, which had been men sitting on one side and women and children on the other, allowed everyone to sit where they chose. Worship was changed from German to English, and a pipe organ was installed. The organ was powered by a gasoline generator and later by electricity when REA arrived in the area.

Somewhere between 1959 and 1960, as the children were practicing for Christmas Eve Services, a fire broke out and completely destroyed the church building. This was indeed a time of severe testing for the congregation. They finally reached the decision that they would start building a new church in the summer of 1960.

In 1923, Peace Lutheran congregation joined the South Dakota District of the Lutheran Church – Missouri Synod. God's blessings indeed have been abundant upon this congregation of our District!

St. John's Lutheran Church, Yankton, South Dakota

By the year 1875 more and more settlers of German descent came into the Yankton area. Thus it was in 1877 that Rosenberg Parish near Mission Hill was organized. At that time it was called Immanuel and was served by Pastor P. Doescher. Martinus and Yankton were preaching stations at that time. After the founding of these three congregations they were served by Pastor Andrew Mueller of Centerville.

Rosenberg Church and parsonage near Yankton and Mission Hill, SD

St. John's Lutheran Church of Yankton was formerly organized by Pastor G. Rumsch in 1882. Pastor Rumsch served this large parish for four years when he accepted a call to Claremont, MN. That same year Martinus Lutheran Church near Utica was organized. Pastor Mueller's travel was done mostly by horse and wagon or buggy. Since he had just graduated from the Seminary he had very little funds. His father loaned him $500 to purchase a Ford. The pastor's annual salary was to be $600 plus three bushels of oats and three bushels of corn from each member of the parish. Because the pastor had no horses, families gave $5 annually to buy gas and oil for the car. There were many hardships but the Lord never slept and kept His Guardian Angels on the alert 24 hours of the day.

The Rosenberg church then closed and members attended Yankton. A cemetery is still maintained at Rosenberg today. In 1921, St. John's and

Martinus became affiliated with the Lutheran Church – Missouri Synod. St. John's also had a Christian Day School which was started in 1947.

As the congregation continued to grow the need for larger facilities became evident. Groundbreaking was then held on April 21, 1968. A $400,000 church and educational unit was to be constructed and work to begin immediately. This was made possible by a loan from the South Dakota District Church Extension Fund in the amount of $300,000. Cornerstone ceremonies were held September 29, 1968. On May 25, 1969, (Pentecost Sunday) the formal dedication service was held with the Reverend Elmer Knoernschild of St. Louis, MO preaching.

St. John's Lutheran Church, Kaylor, South Dakota

The early forefathers of St. John's originally lived in an over-populated section of Germany where they were enticed by many promises and allurements of both the German King and the Russian Czar to settle in southern Russia along the northern shore of the Black Sea and in parts of the Crimea. Being frugal and industrious by nature, and under the abundant blessings of the Lord our God, these German villages in Russia grew and prospered, soon embracing many of the former Russian villages as well. Fine schools and churches were built. It was natural that jealousies and bitterness arose against these German immigrants and promises and concessions made by the government were forgotten. Instead, heavy taxes were imposed upon them, their sons and fathers were drafted for military service in the Russian army and religious freedom was denied them.

They bitterly regretted having to leave their homeland, but sailed for America, the land of freedom. So it was in 1875 that all the inhabitants of an entire village set sail for America and, after 14 days at sea, arrived in New York City. Five days later they reached Yankton-Dakota Territory, which was the terminal of the railroad. From there they headed northeast to Scotland and Kaylor.

The exact date of organization of St. John's is uncertain from the early records but we do know that a group of Lutheran Christians was served regularly as early as 1879 when St. John's was part of the parish of Reverend J.J. Bernthal, together with other groups. St. John's is the mother church of a parish that once included preaching places and later congregations in Avon, Delmont, Scotland, Tripp, Tyndall, Wagner and two known as Zion of Hutchinson and Bon Homme counties. These latter two are no longer in existence. Originally the members met in homes, until a church was built in the 1880's along with a parsonage and school, at a site about a mile south and east of Kaylor. In 1913 this old building was moved into Kaylor. Later a church was purchased from the Evangelical United Brethren in Olivett and moved into Kaylor and placed next to the old church. The original church was eventually torn down. The new church was dedicated on June 9, 1963.

St. John's at one time boasted a Christian Day School (taught by Pastor Ehlen) which flourished for many years. Mention is made in the records of: a teacher Wyneken, son of the famed President C.F.D. Wyneken; a Miss Lydia Treiber, later Mrs. Philip Spomer; and Andrew Voll. The old creamery building served as the school from 1896-1898 with rooms on the second floor being used as living quarters for the teachers.

Pastor Ehlen, along with serving St. John's, served the church at large as synodical visitor, member of the Mission Board, vice-president and as District President from 1912 to 1918. Both he and his wife are buried in the Scotland cemetery. Because of dwindling membership, the congregation was disbanded in March 1999.

Chapter 5
1881-1883

St. John's Lutheran Church, Revillo, South Dakota

In December of 1880, German Lutheran settlers in Grant County met to organize a congregation. The young Reverend Frederick Pfotenhauer (Yellowbank, Minnesota), eager to extend his parish, crossed over the boundary of Minnesota into Dakota Territory and guided these Lutheran brethren in organizing a congregation. The newly formed congregation adopted the name, "St. Paul's Evangelical Lutheran Church." On April 30, 1881, the members of St. Paul's congregation met and accepted the constitution drawn up by Pastor Pfotenhauer.

Soon after, a Sunday School was organized and the first call was extended to Candidate Theodore Hinck, who was installed by Pastor Pfotenhauer on August 13, 1882. Because of the rapid growth of the congregation, it was decided on March 22, 1886 to build a church 1 mile north of Albee on land donated by John Koelle.

Pastor Pfotenhauer of Yellowbank, Minnesota was then elected President of the Lutheran Church – Missouri Synod. (He served in that capacity from 1911 to 1935.) On January 23, 1911, a constitution was adopted and officers elected for the congregation in Revillo. Reverend Nitschke was called to be regular pastor at St. John's along with St. Paul's (of Albee township).

In 1928, St. John's joined the Lutheran Church – Missouri Synod and its name was changed to St. John's Evangelical Lutheran Church – Missouri Synod. In 1962, St. Paul's congregation, after 82 years of organization, accepted the invitation to unite with St. John's. St. John's still maintains the St. Paul cemetery for those who choose to use it. It was after 1978 that a parish agreement was formed between the Bethlehem congregation of Big Tom and St. John's of Revillo to form a joint parish served by one pastor.

Trinity Lutheran Church, Hartford, South Dakota

Evangelical Lutheran Trinity congregation was organized in the year 1881 with 13 families. These families had left Germany to come to America and settled in the Wall Lake township area of South Dakota. Services were first held in various homes. In 1882 the church grounds were beginning to take shape at the present location.

The first church building was erected at a cost of $1,050 and was dedicated in 1882. The building was used for worship services for 24 years and then moved to Crooks. On September 17, 1901 the land where the present church now stands was donated and a church erected in 1906. The cement brick for the church exterior was made on the premises with sand hauled by a team and wagon from Wall Lake. The total cost of the church is thought to be $8,000. The basement was added a few years later and was dug with shovels, pails and horses.

The first schoolhouse was built in 1904 and was used until 1920 when the old parsonage was remodeled and used for Christian Day School. This Day School was organized in 1920 and was closed in 1927. In 1966 stained glass windows were installed in the church. A new fellowship hall has just recently been added to the church as well as a garage near the parsonage.

Immanuel Lutheran Church, Dimock, South Dakota

In the years 1880 and 1881 the first settlers were Schlesische Lutherans from Germany who were affiliated with the Breslov Synod and settled in the Dimock area. These were joined by more Lutherans of German descent from Wisconsin. They were advised by their former pastor in Germany to seek a pastor from the Missouri Synod to serve them. The first Missouri Synod pastor to serve them was the Reverend A. Muller of Marion Junction. Shortly after this the Reverend J. Bernthal of Scotland served them.

It was in 1882 that 23 families organized and formed the Evangelical Lutheran Immanuel Congregation Unaltered Augsburg Confession. The newly established congregation extended a call to Pastor Bernthal of Scotland who accepted its call.

In 1889 the congregation built its own house of worship and laid the cornerstone on second Easter Day. The church was built at a cost of $1,000 and last served as Zion congregation at Stickney. Immanuel also built its own school house in 1903. In 1914 it was decided to build a new church at the cost of $10,000. This cost was underwritten by members before the building of the church started. On April 26, 1914 the cornerstone was laid and on August 30th the new church was dedicated to the glory of God.

It was in 1944 that English services were held once a month. In 1946 the Sunday School was organized. In 1955 Reverend Leonard Eberhard was installed as pastor of the congregation. Pastor Eberhard later served our District as part-time District President while serving Immanuel, Dimock.

Chapter 6
Mid 1880's

Trinity Lutheran Church, Mansfield, South Dakota

Early work among the German Lutheran pioneers was done by Missionary Bernthal who was the first one to come to this vicinity to serve these people. He was one of the so-called traveling missionaries who went from place to place having no definite home.

The first church service in this community was conducted in the Chicago and Northwestern Depot at Northville. Later the services were conducted in various homes. Still later, services were conducted in the school house in Northville Township.

The first missionary to establish a mission-place in this region was Reverend T. Hinck, who came in the year 1882 and made his home in Groton. Because of the large field in which he served, he was able to visit each preaching place only every 4th or 6th week. He would preach as well as stay and instruct children in the catechism and in Christian doctrine.

In the fall of 1886, Candidate George Fischer was called to serve the Mansfield area. He stayed with the William Boekelheide family and served the mission places at Wecota, Rudolph, Aberdeen and Wesley. No early records were preserved, but Pastor George Fischer apparently organized Trinity Congregation shortly after his arrival there. It is generally agreed that the organization took place in the year 1886.

In the spring of 1888, the congregation decided to build a church. There was quite a controversy among the members concerning where the church should be located. Eventually the site was chosen and dedication services were held for the first Trinity Lutheran Church on October 21, 1888.

In September 1892, Candidate F.A. Kiess arrived as Pastor to this new field. He served St. John's of Rudolph as well as St. Paul's of Aberdeen, St. Paul's of Wesley and Immanuel of Wecota (among others). Pastor Kiess, as mentioned in an earlier chapter, was the one who made the missionary trip to the Black Hills and preached to the patrons in a saloon in Deadwood.

It was during Pastor Kiess' ministry that Trinity congregation became a member of Synod in 1894.

NOTE: This excerpt is from the memoirs of pioneer missionary F.A. Kiess titled, "My Experiences in the Mission Field of South Dakota." The booklet by this intrepid, energetic, "sod-busting" man of God illustrates dramatically how "the Word of the Lord grew."

A Keyhole Glimpse

Second Year of My Mission Work in South Dakota.

"My pony named Minnie became sick and could not do the work anymore. Poor Minnie, from the time of that terrible blizzard she began to fail, she was put on pasture and given a rest, well deserved. Hans was put in her place.

In June I went to Synod in Minneapolis and left my young wife with the wife of a neighbor pastor, 45 miles from our home. While there she experienced her first cyclone, while we were at Synod. The cyclone had lifted the church from its foundation, demolished the sheds, but left the parsonage in unharmed condition. God saved the wives of his servants.

At that Synod of the Minnesota and Dakota District I presented five (5) voting congregations to Synod; Mansfield, Northville, Aberdeen, Wecota, and Ashton congregations. Amid cheers and applause they were accepted. The President of the District declared, "Never in the history of Synod were so many congregations presented by one man."

Every missionary had to make a verbal report of his work and accomplishment in his field. So my report was of such a nature to please the Synod to such an extent, that it was unanimously decided to give me an assistant in the person of a student. In September the student arrived and he was a great help to me, supported by the Mission Board.

Some happenings of Sad and Joyous Nature During the Summer, 1893.

"An old mother came to live in South Dakota on the lonesome prairie with her only child, a son, and only relative. The son left one day to find work outside of the state – he never returned. The old mother did not give up hope for his return. She made and remade his bed every day. She kept a few chickens and the neighbors took care of her. A member of my congregation near Wecota, sent his sons with horse and buggy every Sunday morning to bring her to services, whenever we had services, every two weeks. So she was in services on a Sunday in June. The following Sunday there was no service. She must have died on that Sunday or even before, and she would often mention that some day they would find her dead. Neighbors, who had not seen her for several days, but thinking she stayed with the member who always sent for her to go to services, which she sometimes did. Upon investigating they found the poor old mother on bed, dead and decayed. The undertaker could not touch the body but placed it in a coffin with bedding and all. The funeral service was held immediately. Of course the corpse could not be taken into the church but was left in the hearse. After the service, she was interred in her grave. When I returned home I had to leave my books and gown outside because of the offensive odor still in them from the decayed body. It was one of my funerals always imprinted in my memory.

The first year of our marriage my wife would accompany me on my trips every Saturday and Sunday. On one occasion we were driving out west on

Saturday afternoon. The wind was fierce, I had lit my pipe, but the wind blew so terribly that a spark lit on the lap robe and burnt a hole through it and into my wife's dress. She felt the fire and I stopped immediately and extinguished it. The only time I set my wife afire, never there-after.

The members of my congregation would supply us with food to a great extent. We never bought potatoes, and the Dakota potatoes have all the potatoes beaten by far in the world. The potatoes were so cheap, the farmers only dug as many as they needed. The rest were left in the ground. We bought no flour or meat in the winter. One brought a whole pig, another a quarter of beef for Thanksgiving. Meat was cheap, pork was .85 a hundred, wheat .30 and .35. The year 1893 was a year of depression in our country, but fuel was high – hard coal $16.00 a ton, gasoline .25 a gallon, coal oil .20 a gallon, clothing and shoes were high too. Eggs were .05 a dozen, butter .06 a pound. Two bachelors, Jim and Charles, brothers, supplied us with eggs, they were honest-to-goodness neighbors. To prove their honesty, when they discovered they had overcharged us a penny, immediately both came and as poor sinners would repent of accepting too much money and brought the one penny back. Honesty! Charles and Jim loved to come over and spend the lonesome evenings with us. They were quite good musicians and we had some pleasant evenings.

Since I received no support from the mission funds, the Board of Missions declared all money taken in by me in my mission field was my property. All salaries $400.00 per year paid every 12 months, all collections taken in was my property and support. So I turned all collections taken in the second year over to my wife, she purchased a reed organ from the Hinnes Organ Co., Pekin, IL, the balance of our savings since the banks were closed, were frozen up not only in zero temperature, but also in summer heat of 115 in the shade, we buried it in the cellar, no more money buried there-after.

On one of my trips, my wife experienced some unusual things. We stayed with a member who had a one room house, he and his wife and two children, one bed and a trundle bed for the children. Where did we sleep? A ladder led up into the loft of the house. We had to climb up that ladder and once up could not stand erect, but were compelled to undress while on our knees, but oh, how we slept! At another member's house, we had a soft bed in a comfortable bedroom. Soon after we had retired, I noticed that my better half could not go to sleep, but romped around in bed from one side to the other. Upon my question "What's the matter?" She replied, "I believe there are bedbugs in this bed." We made a light and sure enough she was right. I could sleep, for they never touched me, but my wife could not sleep all night. In the morning the lady of the house asked her "Haben dich auch die wanzen gebissen" ("Did the bedbugs bite you?") She answered, "No."

A missionary must be prepared for all kinds of emergencies. Two weeks ahead I had announced confirmation of twelve children, and after the confirmation, celebration of Holy Communion. When I arrived after a trip of 25 miles at the church, what did I find? First, there was a corpse in front of the altar, some old grandmother whom I had given private communion *two weeks before, had passed away. Second, there was in the front seat a young couple ready to enter holy wedlock. Third, five mothers with their babies to be baptized and then there was the confirmation and Holy Communion. What to do first? Should I drop some parts, or go through the entire program? I decided on the latter. At 2 p.m. I was due to preach at Ipswich, and would not get through with all the work here and travel 20 miles to Ipswich. So the first thing I did was to dispatch a young man with a fast horse to go and notify the people to wait for me until 4 p.m. The second on the program was the funeral service with songs and sermon and burial. The third was baptism of the five babies; a song preceded the baptismal service. Fourth, a song for the couple to be married, then the marriage performed. Fifth, examination of the confirmation class, address, song and confirmation. Sixth, confessional service with short address, seventh, regular service with songs and sermon. Eighth, celebration of Holy Communion, all took part, the newly confirmed, their parents, sponsors, the five mothers with babies in arms, the newly married couple, the benediction and song for conclusion ended this never-to-be-forgotten service. We started at 9:30 a.m. and it lasted until 2:30 p.m. After the service we were invited to the home of the young bride's parents which happened to be on my way to Ipswich. In my memorandum I put down that no more has ever been taken in on a single day than this, $186.50, for salary, funeral, baptism, marriage, confirmation and collection. After a sumptuous wedding dinner, I immediately departed for Ipswich and arrived there at 4:30. Everyone remained, I held a short service noticing my voice had given out. Is it a wonder? I remained at Ipswich that night.*

Before I shall go on with the narration of my experiences in the mission field of South Dakota, I will mention the entire field which I covered alone, and the congregations with their pastors of the years 1931 and 1932.

1.	*Mansfield, SD, Reverend C.F. Kellermann – 215 souls.*
	Chelsea, SD, Reverend C.F. Kellermann – 62 souls
2.	*Aberdeen, SD, 13 miles southwest (formerly Rudolph)*
3.	*Aberdeen, SD, Reverend F.J. Graeber – 300 souls*
4.	*Aberdeen, SD, Reverend F.,T. Eggert – 236 souls*
5.	*Ipswich, SD, Reverend R.F. Gaunn*
6.	*Wecota, SD, Reverend A. Szegedin – 138 souls*
7.	*Roscoe, SD, Reverend J.P. Scherf*
8.	*Hot Springs, SD Reverend A.C. Scholtz (Agencies 13C)*
9.	*Lebanon, SD, Reverend Th. Schroeder.*

Hot Springs was only visited by my weighty partner and myself."

Chapter 7

Growth Continues

Zion Evangelical Lutheran Church, Geneseo (rural Milbank), South Dakota

Zion Evangelical Lutheran Church of Geneseo, South Dakota was organized in 1881. Land was deeded to the church by George and Sophia Bear in March of 1895.

According to the books at Emanuel Lutheran Church in Milbank, treasurer G.P. Mueller kept track of every cent that was given to the church. (An examination of the figures suggests that, when a bill needed to be paid, the people must have taken the money from their pockets and given it to the church.) I don't believe I saw in the books that anyone had ever given more than $20.

By August of 1945 the church was very much in need of repair. An

Zion Lutheran Church, Geneseo
(north of Milbank, SD)

estimate of the cost came to be $1,251.67 and did not include the moving of the church to higher ground, the paint and the excavating. So the decision was made to dissolve Zion Lutheran Church.

They sold the church and it was moved to Wilmot and made into a home. The treasurer sent $700 to the District Treasury and retained money to pay off expenses incidental to the sale and for the fencing of the cemetery. The balance was to be sent to the District Church Extension Fund. It was decided that the Zion cemetery should be placed into the trusteeship of Emanuel Lutheran congregation at Milbank unless in the future they would decide to build a church at that same location.

The final service was held on Sunday evening, September 29, 1946.

Bethlehem Lutheran Church, Milbank, South Dakota

Early records indicate that the first services were held in homes of early settlers in the rural Milbank area as well as in some public school house. Not long after, Bethlehem was given ten acres of land for a church building. This was in 1885. On this was erected a parsonage for their Pastor. In the fall of 1900, Bethlehem voted to build a school house on the premises. This building was later disposed of by sale in 1940.

Lutherans near Lake Albert and Big Tom held a meeting September 22, 1882 in the school house for the purpose of organizing an Evangelical Lutheran congregation. As a result of this meeting, Bethlehem Evangelical Lutheran congregation UAC, Grant County, D.T. was formed. The calling of a pastor did not materialize until 1885, when under the guidance of Pastor Pfotenhauer, a joint call was issued by Bethlehem and St. Paul's (Albee) to a Candidate Claus.

(Bethlehem, Milbank) Bethlehem Lutheran Church, Alban Township, Rural Milbank

Today Bethlehem is a joint parish with St. John's of Revillo.

Trinity Lutheran Church, James Township (rural Groton)

The Reverend Dr. F. Pfotenhauer was a busy missionary in the northeast part of South Dakota. It was in July of 1882 that Pastor Pfotenhauer laid the foundation for the Lutheran Church – Missouri Synod congregation at James, South Dakota. It was also during this time that mission work was organized in West Hanson Township and Columbia, South Dakota. In 1884 a parochial school was erected and dedicated at James.

Later, Trinity congregation of James, St. John's of West Hanson Township and St. Paul's of Stratford were served as a joint parish. In 1951 Trinity congregation of James closed its doors and services then were conducted only at Stratford and St. John's, West Hanson.

St. Peter's Lutheran Church, Wentworth, South Dakota

During the years 1877 to 1878 settlers began arriving in the Dakota Territory in the Wentworth area. Arriving from Illinois and Wisconsin, many of these Lutheran settlers were served by Reverend Christian Boettcher, a circuit missionary from the Minnesota District of the Synod. He traveled a large area of Southern Minnesota and Dakotas conducting services for these pioneer settlers.

In the year 1882 a few families in the Wentworth vicinity decided to organize a congregation. The German Evangelical Lutheran St. Peter's congregation was officially organized on September 24, 1882. Reading services were conducted in the absence of an ordained minister. In December of 1883, after having held services in a public school building, the congregation decided to build its own church. They erected the structure that was later used as the parish hall. The church was dedicated in December of 1884.

On August 15, 1886 the congregation made the decision to establish a parochial school. By 1913, over 50 pupils were enrolled in the school and were taught by Pastor Oberheu who was assisted by Ella Oberheu. The parochial school closed in 1936 due to extreme financial problems of the 1930's and difficulty obtaining another teacher.

Pastor A.H. Kuntz served St. Peter's and was paid an annual salary of $300 as well as feed for his horses. It was in 1891 that the congregation decided to join the Lutheran Church – Missouri Synod. It was also that year that the congregation was incorporated. In 1904, the congregation decided that the church facilities were too small and that construction would need to begin on a new church building. In 1924 the congregation began another building venture which resulted in a brick school house being constructed in 1926. It was again in 1950 that the decision was made to build a new church which dedication took place on December 3, 1950. St. Peter's has always been mission minded and during Pastor Alva Pingel's pastorate, a mission congregation, Our Savior of Madison was begun. The St. Peter's pastor served the Madison congregation until 1962, when St. Peter's amalgamated with St. John's of Chester. This arrangement is still in effect today.

St. Paul's Lutheran Church, Stratford, South Dakota

St. Paul's of Stratford was organized in the fall of 1907 and was served by Pastor F.J. Graeber, resident pastor of St. Paul's, Aberdeen. Pastor Graeber would preach at Stratford on Sunday afternoons. His travel was by horse and buggy. He served this congregation for almost 37 years. In 1944 Stratford joined with West Hanson and James congregation, forming a parish. St. Paul's is currently served as a joint parish with Trinity of Mansfield.

Martinus Lutheran Church, Utica, South Dakota

It was the year 1882 when Martinus Lutheran Church of Utica was organized by Pastor G. Rumsch. Services were regularly conducted in the home of Mr. and Mrs. Kietzman. The original church was built and dedicated at the old church site two miles south and a half mile east of the present site. A parochial school was built in 1917 and was open only for one year because of stringent laws, especially in the area of certification. A teacher was forced to quit teaching and the school was discontinued.

The present church was built in the years 1923 and 1924 and dedicated August 31, 1924. The church maintained the cemetery at the old church site. Odessa Lutheran Church, located four miles north of Lesterville, disbanded and on April 2, 1950. Fourteen souls were received at Martinus.

In December 1967 Martinus of Utica and Immanuel of Menno formed a dual parish.

Today, Martinus is served as a joint parish together with St. John of Tyndall.

St. Paul Lutheran Church, Freeman, South Dakota

Immigrants from Southern Russia of German nationality came to Dakota Territory in 1874, settling northwest of Yankton. Synod's Mission Board was concerned about the spiritual welfare of these immigrants and sent out Circuit Riders to explore the possibility of starting a new mission field in this area of South Dakota.

The first pastor to minister to the spiritual needs of these people was the Reverend C.W. Baumhoefner of Scribner, Nebraska. Much of Pastor Baumhoefner's travel was done by horse and buggy. However, he did travel by train to the Freeman, South Dakota area. When he was not able to be there, a layman would often read a prepared sermon and lead in the singing and prayers of the people. Strategic places were picked by Synod to place Circuit-Riders who would minister to the vast area of Dakota.

In 1874, Reverend F. Doescher of Fort Dodge, Iowa became the first resident pastor in South Dakota, which at that time was only a territory. He preached his first sermon in 1875 in the Freeman area, where he organized a rural congregation the following year. The settlers chose the name of Heilbronn, after their village in their homeland. Hence the first Missouri Synod Lutheran congregation was organized in Dakota and became known as Trinity Lutheran Church. (See Chapter 4)

After Reverend Doescher accepted a call out of Dakota a new graduate of the St. Louis Seminary, Ernst Melcher arrived in Dakota in 1878 being ordained and installed at Centerville by Reverend G.E. Friedrich who had arrived the year before.

In 1879 the town of Freeman was founded and families of Lutheran background settled in the new village. Pastor Melcher, now living in Centerville, served this area traveling by horse and buggy. Many hardships were encountered as coyotes and prairie dogs were numerous. He had to carry a pistol to ward off wild animals from injuring him or his ponies. A compass was a necessity in his travels in these wide open prairies.

Pastor Melcher served as many as 17 preaching stations in eight counties traveling a round trip of 400 miles and being gone from home for weeks at a time. In some of the larger gathering of members he would also teach school on days when he wasn't traveling. Under Pastor Melcher's dedicated leadership St. Paul Lutheran Church of Freeman was organized in 1882. Four years after its organization St. Paul acquired some property and built its first church structure. The new structure was dedicated in 1866.

The congregation from its early beginnings realized the need for religious training for its children. A two-story house was built south of the church which served as school and living quarters for the teacher.

South Dakota District Convention, Freeman, SD 5-11, June 1912

Following Pastor Melcher's acceptance of a call to Waverly, Iowa, Pastor Albert Brauer came to serve St. Paul and the entire Freeman area in September of 1889. Pastor Brauer became the first called pastor and served Freeman and Heilbronn as a dual parish. It was June 20-26, 1906 that the South Dakota

District of the Lutheran Church – Missouri Synod was organized in Freeman with 39 pastors, three teachers and 76 congregations forming the new District. J. Adolf Schamber of Freeman had just graduated from St. Louis Seminary and became the first native-born South Dakotan to become a pastor. He signed the Constitution and became a charter member at this Convention. His first preaching assignment was at Britton, South Dakota.

The dual parish of Trinity, Heilbronn and St. Paul, Freeman was served by one pastor, but each congregation supported its own teacher and school.

As these congregations began to grow it became ever more difficult for one pastor to serve both congregations. Trinity of Heilbronn requested to sever connections with St. Paul Freeman in order that each congregation might call its own pastor. They were granted a peaceful release from the dual parish situation on March 7, 1915.

It was in November of 1922 when the Heilbronn congregation asked again to form a dual parish with St. Paul as they were unable to support a pastor and a teacher alone. They agreed to pay half of the pastor's salary but St. Paul, Freeman had the expenses of maintaining the parsonage. This merger was completed and Pastor Gustav Steffen served both congregations. At this time, St. Paul's building, which was built in 1899, was heated by two pot-bellied stoves with stove pipes suspended in mid-air across the ceiling. As the congregation grew it became apparent that the church needed improvements and so the two stoves were removed and a coal furnace was installed in the newly-constructed partial basement.

The need also for modern facilities was necessary at the Lutheran School and so the decision was made to build a new and larger school. Mr. Fred Harr, one of the charter members and very active and dedicated church worker offered a half block of his property free of charge for the school. This offer was accepted and the members made plans to erect a brick building at the cost of $10,000.

In February of 1944, Pastor Eiffort accepted a call to Iowa and the congregation decided to sever connections with the Heilbronn church once again and call its own pastor. The workload for one pastor for two congregations was far too much for adequate shepherding of the number of souls to be served. Regular services were held in both German and English every Sunday.

God continued to bless St. Paul throughout the years so that by October of 1959 the congregation decided to build a new church rather than to remodel or enlarge the old one. More seating was needed for Sunday services as well as additional parking area, etc. In 1961 it was decided to secure a full square block, 300 x 300 feet for the new church. And so it was in January of 1962 the voters decided to proceed with the building of a new church at a cost of

$125,000. Pastor Albrecht conducted groundbreaking services on April 15, 1962. The new church was dedicated on Mother's Day, May 12, 1963.

(NOTE: St. Paul Lutheran School was organized in 1888, the first parochial school in South Dakota and the only Lutheran School to be in continuous operation for over 100 years.)

St. John's Lutheran Church, Wolsey, South Dakota

In the spring of 1883, Reverend Ottomar Cloeter was stationed at Huron, South Dakota and served as Missionary-at-Large. In June of 1884, a communion service was held at Huron and Mr. and Mrs. John Jungemann of Wolsey were among the communicants. Since new Lutheran families had homesteaded in the Wolsey vicinity, Pastor Cloeter decided to move to Wolsey, as the railroad connections were good there.

Since a parsonage hadn't been provided, Pastor Cloeter built one with his own hands. Its dimensions were 12 feet by 16 feet.

The first congregational meeting was held on June 14, 1885. First officers were elected and in the fall of 1886 it was decided to build the first chapel. This chapel was to be 20 feet by 30 feet with 12 foot posts. However, some of the members thought the building should be two feet longer, so it was contracted for $375 dollars and an additional 2 feet would cost $10 more. The decision was made to add the extra two feet. This chapel was used from 1886 until 1907 for worship services and later was used as a Christian Day School. Following Pastor Cloeter's acceptance of a call to Iowa, Pastor Naumann served Wolsey congregation as well as other areas around Wolsey.

It was in 1895 that Reverend F.W. Leyhe accepted a call to the Wolsey congregation. He had just graduated from the seminary in St. Louis. Since there had been a vacancy at Wolsey the parsonage was rented to a bachelor by the name of Ernest Witthoeft for $2 a month. He had a few pieces of furniture, some dishes and a bed, and he shared this home with Reverend Lehye for some time. When Mr. Witthoeft accepted a section foreman job elsewhere, Reverend Lehye was forced to buy his own furnishings. He sent to E.M. Roberts Company for three chairs for 41¢ each, a table for 98¢ (this table was in use in the Leyhe home for the rest of his life), a set of dishes for a few dollars and a frying pan. When the order came, Reverend Lehye didn't have enough money to pay the freight so he had to wait for some time. Not having money for a bed, he put his buffalo robe on the floor, a feather bed and quilt on top and many covers. His salary was $150 per year at Wolsey and the same at Yale. For six months he received $14 at Wolsey and $18 at Yale.

About this time Pastor Leyhe was given a team and buggy by the mission board. He spent $14 for new wheels and axle on the buggy and the rest of his salary took care of him and his horses. The first year of his ministry, Pastor Leyhe traveled 6,432 miles as he served Onida and Agar, 90 miles from Wolsey; Blunt, 70 miles; and Highmore, 50 miles; as well as Yale, Cavour, Iroquois, LaDelle and Huron. The people at Blunt, Highmore and Onida paid him in meat, bread and canned goods. He traveled by horse and buggy for over 22 years. He tried to get to Yale every other week, but sometimes that wasn't possible, as he relates in his own story:

> *"October 23, 1896, the first snow came of 18 inches. Later, more snow came and that winter we had six feet of snow on the level." (Roads were impassable, so he spent some time that winter in Wisconsin with his mother.) "The snow melted and I was in hopes that I could make Yale as I had not been there for a few weeks. So one Saturday morning I took the train to Cavour. That day we had a real thaw and by noon the water was running in rivulets. I tried to hire a livery team to drive to Yale but the livery man flatly refused to let a team that day. He told me that the roads were softening and that by afternoon, no horse would be able to travel the roads. But I must get to Yale. Mr. Maass got me a pair of rubber boots that reached way over my knees. Soon I was on my way to Yale, satchel in hand. All went well until I came to a place in the road where the water had gathered. I thought that I could make it, and I walked into the water and before I realized, my boots were filled with water to the brim. Nothing to do but to walk back to Cavour. But the trial had been made to go to Yale.*

> *"I intended to take the train back to Wolsey on Monday morning, but there was no train until Thursday morning. I took that train to Huron and arriving there I was told that there would be no train for some time to come. I had some 25¢ in my pocket then that would not keep me very long, so I decided I had to walk to Wolsey following the railroad track. All went well until I came to the Halfway Slough. The wind was blowing from the north and I could see from a distance how the water beat up against the track spurting up into the air. When I came to the place I really did not know if I ought to wade through the spurting water or not, but I made it without getting very wet.*

> *"How happy I was to see Wolsey looming up in the distance. But my happiness was shortly turned to sorrow for when I walked down the hill towards Cane Creek I noticed that the whole bottom was flooded, even the track had been removed from its bed and had been fastened with heavy chains to the telegraph posts. What now? Turn back now with only a quarter in my pocket? So I risked to walk the wet slippery ties. All went well until I came to a place where a number of ties were missing. The space was not very large and so I tried to jump, I struck the next tie, but lo, it was loose and I went into the icy water up to my chest. After that I did not care what happened. Men were working at the bridge to save it from going out and how they laughed to see me coming across the floating track. I did not feel much like joking as I was chilled to the bone. The next day I was so stiff that I could hardly lift a foot and the next Sunday I could hardly make the stairs of the pulpit. It took a long time to get over the effects of that trip."*

Many and varied were the hardships that Pastor Leyhe endured during those early years while serving in the Wolsey area.

Pastor Leyhe was united in marriage with Miss Anna Kohlmeyer of Wolsey of May 26, 1915.

St. John's of Wolsey joined the Synod in 1900. Pastor Leyhe at that time served two regular congregations as well as four preaching stations, 243 communicant members, 51 voting members and one Lutheran School taught by the pastor with 12 pupils.

Pastor Leyhe was elected President of the South Dakota District of the Lutheran Church – Missouri Synod in 1921. He continued serving in this capacity until 1936. Three South Dakota District conventions have been held at St. John's, Wolsey – 1910, 1930 and 1945.

It was in April of 1948 that Pastor Leyhe retired as pastor of St. John's congregation. He had served for nearly 53 years – all of them at St. John's, Wolsey. He departed this life on August 5, 1950 and was laid to rest in St. John's cemetery.

In 1950 it was decided to build a new church instead of remodeling the old one as soon as funds became available. Groundbreaking took place in 1958 for the new church/school building. This new beautiful church was dedicated to the glory of God on June 7, 1959. St. John's has over the years had a Lutheran School at various times showing the value that they placed on teaching the children the truth of God's Holy Word.

Zion Lutheran Church, White, South Dakota

The history of Zion Evangelical Lutheran Church of White begins in 1884 – the same year that the city of White was being settled. Preliminary plans for a church were laid in 1896 and the Evangelical Lutheran Zion's Church of White, South Dakota was formed in 1897. The Reverend R. Polzin, pastor of St. Paul's Evangelical Lutheran Church of Argo Township and Trinity Lutheran of Hendricks, Minnesota assisted the German immigrants in making plans to form a congregation at White. Articles of Incorporation were filed with the State of South Dakota in 1897 and thus the start of Zion Lutheran of White. Dedication of the new church was held in September of 1897. Pastor R. Polzin was called to serve the newly-formed congregation as its first pastor. He served until 1898 while also serving the congregations of St. Paul's at Argo and Trinity Lutheran of Hendricks, Minnesota.

The education of the young was a primary concern of the Lutherans who formed this three-point parish. To meet the needs of educating the young, a small frame schoolhouse was built in the fall of 1912 located on the church grounds in Argo. Reverend Atrops was the teacher for the school. In those early days the confirmands attended school daily to receive their religious instruction before being confirmed.

Sometime later the relationship between the Argo and Hendricks congregations was dissolved. It was therefore in the late 1940's and early 1950's that a relationship was formed with First English Lutheran of Aurora. In the 1970's Zion and First English formed a dual parish – a relationship which still exists to this day.

In the early 1950's Pastor Boerger served the congregation. Pastor Boerger was married while he served here. An interesting paragraph stands out in the minutes of the August 4, 1952 congregational meeting. It states that a motion was made and carried to allow Reverend Boerger (through Sunday) to go to Detroit to get married and go on a honeymoon.

Several interesting resolutions were adopted at the April 17, 1956 Voters' Assembly meeting as well. These resolutions were:

> "Whereas, it has become a habit of many of our members to insist upon sitting in the rear of our church, and thereby compelling mothers with small children to sit far to the front, and whereas, this causes embarrassment when children become restless; therefore be it resolved that we urge our members who do not have small children to sit towards the front; and that we instruct our ushers to assist in carrying out this Resolution. Secretary moves adoption. Whereas several persons have asked to use our church organ; and, whereas it would not be advisable to have the organ used without proper supervision; therefore be it resolved that all who wish to practice on our organ, except our regular organist, inform the pastor or the regular organist of the time at which they will use the organ.

> "That we grant members of our congregation free use of our organ, but that non-members are asked to pay $1 an hour for the use of the organ. Secretary moves adoption. Whereas, our church facilities are sometimes used for functions not under the sponsorship of our congregation; and whereas, these functions are not under the censorship of our pastor, and, whereas speakers may at times use language which is unbecoming to God's house and offensive to Christians; therefore, we instruct our pastor and the Board of Elders to draw up regulations to govern the use of our facilities and to present them at the next meeting."

It was in October of 1973 that the Voters' Assembly made the decision giving women the right to vote and the opportunity to hold certain offices in the congregation. The voting age was also lowered to 18 years of age.

Trinity Lutheran Church, White Lake, South Dakota

The first services were held in the White Lake area in 1883. It was in 1884 that St. Martin's Lutheran Church (White Lake) was organized. This was the first church building dedicated in the White Lake community.

St. John's Lutheran Church (Crystal Lake) was organized and its first church building was dedicated in 1888. In 1913-1914 St. John's Lutheran Church (Gales Township) was built and the congregation was officially organized in 1914. St. John's then organized and started a Christian Day School in 1922. A new church building was erected at Crystal Lake in 1930.

It was in 1944 that St. John's Christian Day School closed.

In 1954, St. Martin's, St. John's (Crystal Lake) and St. John's (Gales Township) were merged into Trinity Lutheran Church of White Lake. In 1955 Trinity Lutheran Church was completed and dedicated. Trinity celebrated its 100th anniversary in 1984.

St. Paul's Lutheran Church, Plankinton, South Dakota

1883 marked the first services held in the Plankinton area. It was not until 1910 that St. Paul's Lutheran Church was organized. The original church building was dedicated in 1913.

The dedication of the current church building was held in 1963.

It was in 1985 that St. Paul's celebrated its 75th anniversary.

St. John's Lutheran Church, Agar, South Dakota

The Reverend Ottomar Cloeter was stationed at Huron, SD as Missionary-at-Large in the spring of 1883. Hearing of several Lutheran families who had homesteaded in the Wolsey vicinity he moved to Wolsey and there began serving the people of that area. Pastor Cloeter, traveling by foot, saw the need to serve people in the Agar area and began serving what is now known as St. John's Lutheran congregation of Agar. This was in 1885 when he traveled to this section of the country from Wolsey by foot. After finishing services at Agar (at that time known as Waterford), he would walk to Blunt. He also traveled out to the Black Hills with the intention of starting some preaching stations there. Pierre and Rapid City were two of the cities he visited, but he was not successful in establishing any permanent stations at either of those places during his time of service in this field.

After Pastor Cloeter left, Pastor Justus Naumann started serving a group of Lutherans in the Agar area in 1890. He was also in charge of the congregation north of Harrold including work as far north as Gettysburg and some of the other congregations in the vicinity.

Pastor H. Ohldag was the first resident pastor of St. John's congregation. He was a candidate of the St. Louis Seminary. It was under Pastor Ohldag's leadership that the congregation was formally organized. After Pastor Ohldag accepted a call in the late 1890's Pastor Leyhe from Wolsey served Agar coming out once every six weeks for preaching and serving people with the ministry of the Word and Sacraments.

St. John's Lutheran Church, Agar (1/2 mile east of Agar)

It was in January of 1947 that the church building was moved to its present location in the town of Agar. In 1948 Pastor O.D. Brack of Otto, Texas was called to serve the Gettysburg congregation as well as Agar. He also began preaching services at Onida. Pastor Brack served the South Dakota District in various congregations as well as District Archivist and Chaplain to the Sioux Falls Hospitals for many years. He still serves as Chaplain to the Hospitals at the time of this writing.

The members of St. John's were served faithfully by many pastors over the years until the present time.

Zion Lutheran Church, Canistota, South Dakota

In March of 1880 the Reverend Andrew Mueller, Missionary-at-Large for Dakota Territory, came to Canistota. His first service was held in the home of Mr. Conrad Kirchner.

On Easter Sunday of 1885 the people of Canistota formally organized Zion Evangelical Lutheran Church with about 20 members signing the constitution. The first pastor was Philipp Laux. He was also the teacher in the new parochial school.

It was in 1890 that a new church building was erected. The cornerstone was laid on May 26, 1892. Easter of 1905 Pastor A.F. Breihan, later to become District President, was installed as pastor of Zion.

In 1912 Zion formerly joined the Lutheran Church – Missouri Synod. In 1914 a new schoolhouse was built.

For some years Zion and St. John's of Montrose formed a dual parish.

Throughout the years God has blessed the members of Zion with faithful pastors and teachers who boldly proclaimed God's Word to a faithful people who served, and continue to serve their God and the people of the Canistota area.

Trinity Lutheran Church, Yale, South Dakota

Before 1883 the early pioneers of what later was to be Trinity Lutheran Church of Yale attended public worship in a mission station in Huron. In 1883 Pastor O. Cloeter served the people and held services first in the Fiecke schoolhouse and later in the Neiling school north of the Ulrich farm.

In the year 1885 a few of the members met with Pastor Cloeter and organized Trinity Lutheran congregation of Yale.

When Pastor Cloeter accepted a call away from the Wolsey/Yale area Pastor Justus Naumann served followed by Pastor F.W. Leyhe who served Yale until 1907. It was during this time that the church was built in the country on a plot of land donated by Carl Kuehl and dedicated on January 28, 1900. This church was built at a cost of $1,091.79 and measured 28 x 40 feet.

At a Voters' Meeting in 1934 the following is of interest:

> "The 'Feed' situation was discussed. There was hay, etc., for the pastor's cows and chickens. I remember either Pastor Israel or Pastor Rausch had a cow that would eat most anything and summers when we had Vacation Bible School he would keep part of our lunch to give to the cow! Motion was made to clean up the cemetery."

Records further indicate the following:

> "In June it was decided to 'fix up' the parsonage including some screens and a door. Summer school, which what is today called Vacation Bible School, was to be held in the school at Yale. It was suggested that communion announcements be made on the two Sundays preceding communion or some night the week before. It was also suggested that church services start promptly at the set time (wonder who was dragging their feet here?) Motion was made and seconded that Trinity members clean the church alphabetically."

On January 19, 1941 a special meeting was held to discuss moving the church to Yale. A motion was made to move the church with the following vote taken: pro: 12; contrary: 17. Motion was then made that the church be moved to Yale if enough money could be raised to cover all expenses. This carried. Obviously enough money must have been raised because the church did indeed move to Yale.

The congregation was always mission-minded. In December of 1953 a motion was passed that the congregation would investigate the possibility of starting a mission at Iroquois.

In 1954 this mission opened up in Iroquois with a number of members transferring from the Yale congregation to Iroquois to serve as the nucleus for a new church. In 1956 a new church building was dedicated.

An interesting note in the history of the congregation shows that Pastors didn't make all of the decisions about even the robes that they wore. *"A leak in the roof was repaired and Pastor Ernst was given permission to wear surplice and stole if he wished."* As the years continued and the population in the Yale area decreased, the congregation saw fit to close its doors at the end of 2004. Many of its furnishings were given to the new mission church, Risen Savior Lutheran Church, Tea, South Dakota. And so these Christian brothers and sisters continue to share what God had given them so that His word could continue to be proclaimed in areas which were growing and where people were coming to hear that Word.

St. Peter's Lutheran Church, Clayton (Emery), South Dakota

The areas between Yankton and Freeman in Hutchinson County were now being served by Lutheran pastors. But as the area continued to grow, farmers moved into the areas west and north of Freeman. Many of these were Lutheran Christians who were interested in also being served. Pastor F. Doescher, who had moved to Dakota Territory in 1874 and was serving eight counties in southeastern South Dakota, began work in the Clayton area. However due to poor health he accepted a call to Texas. Candidate Ernst F. Melcher was installed at Centerville in 1878 and continued the work of spreading the Gospel. He later moved to Freeman and continued working this entire area until 1889. A traveling missionary, a candidate, by the name of Andrew Mueller was ordained and installed at Centerville in 1879 and served 12 mission stations in southeastern South Dakota. Clayton was one of those missions. St. Peter's later became a permanent preaching station in 1881. St. Peter's was formally organized under a constitution in June of 1886.

The first services and church meetings were held in the homes of members and later in the public school. In 1898 St. Peter's congregation accepted an acre of land as a gift from Johann and Anna Langle. At the same time they purchased an additional acre in the same section for the sum of $15. This site in Section 26 of Clayton Township, Hutchinson County has been the home of St. Peter's Lutheran Church for these past many years. St. Peter's was then incorporated in 1899 and laid its first cornerstone that same year.

As the congregation grew, a special interest among the members was in also providing a Christian education for the children. It was decided to build a school in 1902, which was then dedicated on November 30, 1902.

St. Peter's Lutheran Church, Clayton-Lutheran School
(horse barn in background) sometime after 1912

During the early years of the congregation only one congregational meeting was held per year. As the congregation grew and the business increased, the members decided to hold meetings every three months. Money for the pastor's salary was collected from members quarterly and he was paid at that time. This system for paying the pastor was in use for many years.

It was in 1915 that St. Peter's Lutheran Church joined in membership with the Synod of Missouri, Ohio and other States. In 1937 one English service was held per month in addition to the German services. It's interesting to note the following:

> *"In 1936 the Ladies Aid purchased a Delco light plant for use in the church, school, and parsonage. The installation, wiring and fixtures were all paid for by the ladies through contributions, bazaars and other fundraisers. Until this time, hanging lamps lighted the church for the few evening services held. Candles were used to decorate and light the Christmas tree. To guard against fire while the tree candles were lit, two men stood by with long poles wrapped with a wet cloth on the end, ready to extinguish any sudden flare up. The light plant was used to generate electricity until 1947 when the Rural Electric Association began to serve the area."*

In January of 1948 the congregation decided to build a new church. Work was begun that summer with members providing most of the labor. The cornerstone ceremony was held on October 3, 1948. Dedication took place on June 19, 1949.

With the building of the new church came also the time to decide on seating arrangements for the congregation. The old tradition called for men on one side and women on the other with children in the front and the young people already confirmed seated in the balcony. The old seating arrangement came to an end and families were encouraged to sit together for worship services. It was then in 1982 that a dual parish arrangement was worked out with St. John's Lutheran Church of Emery. Since that time the two congregations have been one parish served by one pastor.

St. John's Lutheran Church, Howard, South Dakota

St. John's Lutheran Church of Howard, South Dakota was organized in 1882 by a group of German Lutheran pioneers who had settled in Howard and Miner County. In 1883 Pastor H. Kumpf served many of the settlers holding Christian services in the homes. In 1884 the Missouri Synod continued the mission endeavors that had been started by the Iowa Synod in this area.

Records indicate that St. John's incorporated as a congregation in 1887 and became affiliated with the Lutheran Church – Missouri Synod at that time.

In 1887 St. John's purchased lots just north of the present church building and there built its church. The congregation then extended a call to Reverend Christian Meyer in April of 1892 who became the first resident pastor. The congregation became a member of the South Dakota District of The Lutheran Church – Missouri Synod at the Freeman Convention in 1906. During the years 1892-1921 a Lutheran school was in operation at the congregation. This was comprised of grades 1-8. Many of the children came from as far away as Lane and boarded at the parsonage in order to attend the Lutheran School.

As the congregation grew, it was time to think about building a new church. Thus in 1910 work was begun on a new church building. The cornerstone was laid on November 13 of that same year. The church was dedicated in May of 1911 and Reverend A.A. Breihan (then President of the South Dakota District of The Lutheran Church – Missouri Synod) preached the sermon. This was the first entire English service for a Missouri-Synod Lutheran church in the South Dakota District.

From the years 1921-1937, St. John's was the largest congregation in the South Dakota District of The Lutheran Church – Missouri Synod.

St. John's Lutheran Church, Columbia, South Dakota

The history of St. John's Lutheran Church goes back to 1882. Pastor T. Hinck, of the Missouri Synod, (Circuit Rider in the Dakotas and founder of many flourishing congregations held in the northeast corner of the state), began efforts in the Columbia area. The first services were held in a little school house located on the northeast corner of Section 31 in Brainard Township.

Pastor Hinck served the Columbia community until 1886.

A constitution was written and an organized congregation was formed on August 14, 1887. Three acres of land were given by Carl Engel for a church site and cemetery five miles north and one mile west of Columbia. In 1888 a small barn, 12 x 16 was built for $23.98. The first parsonage was purchased for $105. This house was located in Columbia but later moved to the elected church site.

In the year 1899 Columbia and Hecla congregations united and Pastor C.E. Bode was called from Ellendale, North Dakota. Pastor Bode was the first resident pastor of St. John's. Pastor Bode, with the help of his daughter, held parochial school in their home.

St. John's is now served by the pastor from Our Savior, Aberdeen.

St. Paul's Lutheran Church, Aberdeen, South Dakota

On January 5, 1888, St. Paul's Evangelical Lutheran Church of Aberdeen, South Dakota was organized in the home of Mr. and Mrs. Herman Janecke with five voting members. Services for the small congregation were held in several homes for almost 16 years.

Two lots were purchased in the middle of the block facing Seventh Avenue, S.W. for $200. The first church building was dedicated on October 18, 1903.

In January of 1909, the congregation decided to erect a larger church which would provide space for a Christian Day School. The two lots on the corner of south Third Street and Seventh Avenue S.W. were bought for $2,500. In September of 1911, a Christian Day School was started with about 22 children enrolled. Pastor Graeber taught school for one year and Mr. R.F. Lenthaeuser was "Schullehrer" for the next three years. The school was later closed during World War I due, in part, to anti-German feelings.

The present church building was erected and dedication services were held on March 24, 1974.

St. John's Lutheran Church, Aberdeen, South Dakota

Thirteen miles southwest of Aberdeen, South Dakota in Brown County stands our congregation known as St. John's Lutheran Church which was organized in the early spring of 1888. Pastors such as Hinck, Pfotenhauer, Fischer, Ferber all served this congregation as Circuit Rider or Missionary. After its organization, Pastor Fischer served until 1889, G. Ferber from 1889-1892 and F.A. Kiess from 1892-1897. It was during Pastor Kiess' term of service that the first building was erected by the members of the congregation and dedicated to the glory of God in 1896.

In 1913, St. John's joined the Evangelical Lutheran Synod of Missouri, Ohio and other States. Pastor Waack taught in the Lutheran School having, on occasion, over 40 children in attendance.

It was during the ministry of Pastor James Kunze (1958-1961) that a Lutheran school was opened. Lois Krueger became the first teacher.

It was in May of 1976 that a formal parish agreement was made with St. Paul's of Aberdeen. St. John's, since that time, has been served by the pastor from St. Paul's Lutheran Church in Aberdeen.

St. John's Lutheran Church, West Hanson, South Dakota

St. John's Lutheran Church of West Hanson (near Groton) was organized in the fall of 1888. As early as 1883 a traveling missionary, Reverend T. Hinck conducted services in the Sunshine School. In 1884 the Reverend Metz continued this work. In the fall of 1888 the first church building was erected and dedicated to the service of God. At the first congregational meeting held after the dedication, the congregation officially organized under the name of St. John's Evangelical Lutheran Church. Pastor Metz, who was still serving the congregation, then became its first pastor.

In the year 1911 a new church was dedicated to accommodate the growing population of the church. It was during this year, (1911) that the congregation numbered 212 communicants with over 70 voting members.

In 1943, Stratford, Hanson and James became one parish and called as their pastor Reverend A.H. Birner.

On April 27, 1955 a fire of unknown origin completely destroyed the Hanson church. The former James Church was then purchased and moved on to the old church site. It was dedicated to the glory of God on November 20, 1955.

St. John's held its last service on January 26, 1969.

Immanuel Lutheran Church, Wecota, South Dakota

In 1882 Pastor Hinck gathered together scattered German Lutherans in the area of what is now Wecota, South Dakota. First services were held in homes of members.

In 1885 before the church's organization, the Tieman family lost two children, who were buried on their own land. In 1893 the Ziesemeier family lost a set of twins, who were also buried near the Tieman children. Later other graves were added. Mr. Tieman donated two acres of the land to the mission for a cemetery. A warranty deed was registered to Immanuel Congregation on November 6, 1905.

Under the leadership of Missionary Ferber the group organized Immanuel Congregation in 1888. The first house of worship was an abandoned building from somewhere west. Reverend William Meyer came to Immanuel as its first resident pastor.

It was in 1903 that the need for a larger house of worship was felt. In March of 1904 a contract was let to a Mr. Frolick of Aberdeen who would receive 27¢ an hour for his labor while his helper received 20¢ an hour. The members assisted Mr. Frolick in the building. The new church was dedicated sometime in August of 1904. The old building was then used for a church schoolhouse. The congregation was incorporated on January 20, 1920.

St. Martin's Lutheran Church, Alexandria, South Dakota

St. Martin's Lutheran Church goes back to the time of the adoption of its Constitution on October 7, 1888. However, Lutheran church services were held in this vicinity as early as 1879.

The first Lutheran service was conducted by Pastor Melcher in the home of Christ Elfert in the Spring of 1879. Another missionary (of whom the founders of the congregation spoke with affection and gratitude) was Pastor Andrew Mueller. Under God's gracious guidance St. Martin's Evangelical Lutheran congregation in Hanson County, South Dakota was organized as a congregation on October 7, 1888.

In 1899 an important milestone was reached when the congregation built its first house of worship. The building was located eight and 1/2 miles southeast of Alexandria and served as its worship center until the year 1931 when the present property located in Alexandria was purchased. The German language was used almost exclusively until the time when Reverend E. Dewald came to serve as pastor in 1916. Prior to 1931 a group known as the Fairview congregation worshipped in the "Wolf Schoolhouse" nine miles north and a 1/2 mile east of Alexandria. This group met together with the members of St. Martin's in order that they might amalgamate into one congregation. It was decided to disband the Fairview congregation and form one congregation with St. Martin's. Each group contributed $100 toward the purchase price of $1,500 for the church. The church was dedicated on September 6, 1931. The old cemetery where many of the early members of the congregation are at rest may be seen today near the site where the old church once stood, southeast of Alexandria. Today St. Martin's and Trinity of Spencer form a dual parish.

Emanuel Lutheran Church, Milbank, South Dakota

Shortly after the Dakota Territory was open for homesteading in the 1870's many German immigrants came to northeastern South Dakota for settlement. Many of these settlers were of Lutheran background. As such, they sought spiritual guidance from traveling missionaries who were serving this area. The first Lutheran Missionary of record was Pastor Pfotenhauer who lived some 13 miles east of Milbank in Minnesota. Pastor Pfotenhauer traveled back and forth and served today what is our Emanuel congregation. He became President of the Lutheran Church – Missouri Synod in 1911, a position he held until 1935.

District Convention held at Emmanuel, Milbank, June 15-21, 1921

It was on May 5, 1889 that a meeting was held for the purpose of organizing a congregation. It took as its name, "German Emanuel Evangelical Lutheran Church of the Unaltered Augsburg Confession in Milbank, South Dakota." A later meeting was held on June 2, 1889 and a constitution was adopted.

In the Fall of 1907 the congregation completed its original church building which was dedicated on October 27th of that same year. The cost was reported at $3,952.41.

Under God's blessing the congregation continued to grow. In the summer of 1957 the present church and educational wing were completed.

The pre-school was started on October 1, 1979 and is still in existence today.

God continues to bless our Emanuel Congregation as it faithfully serves Him in this area of our District.

Immanuel Lutheran Church, Menno, South Dakota

You've already heard the names of Pastor F. Doescher who began serving in the area around Menno in 1874 and Pastor G.E. Friedrich who served as missionary in 1878.

In 1879 Pastor E.F. Melcher. a graduate of St. Louis Seminary, served the area of Menno, Heilbronn and Freeman, South Dakota with services being held in the homes of various Lutheran Christians. As you can imagine, covering this large an area caused many hardships and difficulties in traveling. Often a "Lesegottesdienste" – a layman would read a prepared sermon from a sermon book along with group singing and prayer.

In 1888 a Lutheran church was built in Menno, South Dakota. At that time all Lutheran pastors, regardless of synodical affiliation were able to conduct services. When Pastor Melcher accepted a call out of the area, a split in the congregation came as a result of difference of opinion in doctrine. Friedens Peace Lutheran Church was then built by members that left the first church. November 19, 1889 under the guidance of Pastor Albert Brauer, Immanuel Lutheran Congregation was organized with a membership of 90 baptized souls. This organized congregation joined the Lutheran Church – Missouri Synod in 1891 which at that time also served Freeman and Heilbronn. The first church building was destroyed by fire caused by lightning in the Spring of 1897 and was replaced that same year.

> *"Heat was provided by a large pot-bellied wood burning stove, which needed faithful attention to keep it fired up, and still was very uneven heat. Wood and coal were carried in and ashes had to be carried out. Men sat on the right side of the church, women on the left. Tradition was for the women to wear a hat or some type of head cover. Communion was held four times a year. Men communed first and then the women."*

The early settlers were very concerned about a Christian education for their children. Thus a parochial school was built to the south of the church in 1904. Pastor Rudolph served as teacher to these children, teaching classes in German. Reading and writing were taught in addition to Bible history and catechism. After the parochial school was closed in 1913, the school was later used for confirmation school held all day on Saturdays. Later the school also served as classrooms for Sunday School.

English services were introduced to the congregation in 1939. This was also the year of the celebration of the 50th anniversary of the congregation. Shortly thereafter the pot-bellied wood-burning stove was replaced with a floor furnace. Families also began sitting together during the worship services.

In July of 1945 Immanuel congregation was presented the proposition from Peace Lutheran congregation (Iowa Synod) in regard to buying their church property. The decision was made to proceed with the purchase of the property thus increasing the seating capacity by about 50. On Sunday, August 26, 1945 members of Immanuel worshipped for the first time in their newly acquired church. The church, complete with all furnishings, comfortably seats 200 and was purchased together with a nine-room parsonage, a 30 x 18 foot schoolhouse and a large barn from the one-time Peace Lutheran Church for $5,000. Forty members of the former Peace congregation joined Immanuel Lutheran Church. In 1953 an addition was built on to the parish hall which included an enlarged kitchen, a utility room and two bathrooms. A new furnace was installed in 1960. In December of 1967, a dual parish was formed with Martinus Lutheran Church of Utica, South Dakota following Pastor William Wendling's departure to Houston, TX.

Zion Lutheran Church, Sioux Falls, South Dakota

Early in the 1870's a number of German Lutherans, especially a group from Mecklenberg, Germany settled near Wall Lake in Minnehaha County. A decade later a larger group located in Sioux Falls. Because missionaries in the southeastern corner of the state had to travel so far in order to provide worship service opportunities for the Lutheran Christians, Sioux Falls became a preaching station being served out of Centerville by the Reverend Andrew Mueller. He conducted his first service in Sioux Falls in the spring of 1880.

On July 16, 1882 the Reverend E. Stark of Trinity Lutheran Church, Wall Lake Township, was called to serve the preaching station in Sioux Falls. In 1889 the Minnesota-Dakota District purchased a lot at 618 South Spring for $1,200. The Reverend G. Buscher was installed as the first resident pastor on August 7, 1889. Zion Lutheran congregation was formally organized on October 1, 1889.

During the next year the newly organized congregation was incorporated and two years later Zion joined the Missouri Synod (then known as The Evangelical Lutheran Synod of Missouri, Ohio and Other States.)

These were happy and prosperous times for the growing Zion congregation. The city numbered some 15,000 residents. Then came the panic of 1893. Businesses closed, families moved away, and Zion lost 1/3 of its total membership. Of the original 30 charter members, only eight remained in 1895.

It was during Pastor Pasche's term as pastor of Zion congregation that a Lutheran School was organized. Teacher Henry Hartman was called to teach the 20 students. In 1913, 43 children were enrolled. This was the highest number attained in the school's existence. Because of limited room for expansion, as well as the noise of traffic on Minnesota Avenue, it was felt for quite some time that a new location would be desirable. In 1948 the congregation purchased 6 lots on Spring Avenue between 22nd and 23rd Streets for $7,000. Three years later the architectural firm of Harold Spitznagel and Associates was engaged to draw plans for a church and parish hall. This plan was accepted by the congregation in 1952.

Groundbreaking ceremonies were held on October 25, 1953 with cornerstone laying ceremonies on May 16, 1954. On March 27, 1955 the new church edifice (constructed at a cost of close to $300,000) was dedicated.

Peace Lutheran Church, Hecla, South Dakota

The history of Peace Lutheran Church dates back to the time when the first settlers, coming from Wisconsin and Illinois, set foot on the soil of the township. Many are the stories of privation, hardships, and dangers of those early days. When raging blizzards mercilessly swept over the treeless and roadless prairies, there were no modern facilities to summon help in case of sudden sickness. Yet the Lord protected these pioneers in their adversities.

The first Missouri Synod Lutheran services in this community were held in Schoolhouse Number 2 on May 11, 1887. Pastor C.C. Metz of Groton conducted the first service and administered the Sacrament of Holy Baptism. This congregation marks as its founding date 1889 – the same year South Dakota was admitted to the Union as a State. Pastor H. Mundt became resident pastor of the Sand Lake (Columbia) congregation and it was under his leadership and direction that Evangelical Lutheran Church of Divine Peace came into being on October 13, 1889. In 1899 the Columbia-Hecla congregations united and called Pastor Bode from Ellendale, North Dakota to serve as pastor.

On May 28, 1901 the laying of the first foundation stone for the church was observed. It was with great joy that on July 14, 1901 the members gathered to dedicate their new church to the glory of God and for the preaching of the pure word and sacraments.

On July 22, 1912 the church edifice was completely demolished as a result of a cyclone. The congregation did not draw back, but set its sights on a new church building for the worship of its God. So it was on the 22nd day of June 1913 that they were permitted to dedicate a new and larger place of worship.

In September of 1937, combination German-English services were held every other Sunday. This gave the younger generation an English service.

Zion Lutheran Church, Hurley, South Dakota

On June 8, 1898 a group of Lutherans organized themselves as a congregation and joined the Lutheran Church – Missouri Synod. This congregation worshipped five miles west of Hurley for some 64 years.

For 44 years Zion was served by the pastors of Centerville. In 1942 Zion united with Bethesda Lutheran of Marion to become one parish served by the pastor of Marion, South Dakota. Zion reunited with First English of Centerville in 1976 and remains in this relationship yet today.

The present church was dedicated on July 29, 1962. It was purchased for $2,000 and moved to town. The

Zion Lutheran Church, Hurley, SD - Building was the last "Heilbronn" church.

church had been the "Heilbronn Church" located southwest of Freeman. God has been good in extending His manifold blessings on the members of Zion for over 100 years!

Chapter 8
1890-1900's

Trinity Lutheran Church, Corona, South Dakota

Trinity Lutheran Church of Corona, South Dakota was organized April 13, 1890. Worship was held in the Kilborn #4 Schoolhouse for four years. Pastor E.Th. Claus of Milbank served as visiting pastor until July of 1890. Since then, various pastors have served Trinity.

Trinity Lutheran Church, Corona, SD

Trinity congregation made plans to build a church and adopted a constitution in March of 1898. It had its own Lutheran School where confirmation was held in the Fire hall in Corona. On June 4, 1899 the congregation was incorporated. It was during the years of 1910-1912 that the German Church constitution was translated into English and services were held in homes because German could not be preached in public.

In 1947, Centennial Lutheran Church of Wilmot was organized and joined Trinity and Christ churches in one parish. In 1978 a dual parish was formed with Wilmot – an agreement which is still in existence today.

Trinity continues, under God's blessings to proclaim the word and administer the sacraments boldly for the salvation of souls!

Zion Lutheran Church, Mitchell, South Dakota

As early as 1881 pastors and missionaries that were affiliated with the Lutheran Church – Missouri Synod were preaching the Gospel of Jesus Christ in Mitchell. This preaching was done in English as well as German. The official minutes of the congregation were also recorded in both languages.

Zion was founded November 27, 1892. The first resident pastor was Pastor Martin Abraham according to Minnesota-Dakota District reports. In 1907 the congregation numbered 80 souls with 11 voting members.

Prior to 1910, services were conducted in homes and rented churches. The church located at 822 East 1st Avenue was dedicated in 1910. The building was purchased from the Congregational Church for $400 and moved at a cost of $300. This building was torn town in 1981.

In 1928 it was reported that the membership had increased from 43 to 86. This moved the congregation to purchase three lots at 3rd and Capitol in 1945. At that time this was farmland. On July 12, 1953 Pastor John Lutze officiated at the dedication of a new church. The construction cost was $225,214.52.

On May 20,1962 the educational unit was dedicated. Zion continues to minister faithfully to the people of the Mitchell area.

First English Lutheran Church, Parker, South Dakota

First English Lutheran Church of Parker was organized in October of 1892 as the Evangelical Immanuel Lutheran Congregation. A constitution was drawn up and adopted at that time.

The first pastor to serve the congregation was the Reverend N. Bohsen who lived in Parker and served a rural congregation near Hurley. Most of the pastors serving during the early years were vacancy pastors from other congregations.

In 1960 when a new pastor was called, First English of Parker and Trinity Lutheran of Hartford joined together to form one parish. Pastor K.L. Johnson served this parish until 1972. The Parker-Hartford parish was dissolved as of November 12, 1975. Discussions were held with Hurley, Centerville and Marion concerning realignment of parishes. It was decided that First English of Parker and Bethesda of Marion would become a dual parish. This became reality in 1976. This arrangement is still in existence today.

Zion Lutheran Church, Waubay, South Dakota

In 1888, Missionaries F. Pfotehhauer and C. Metz started conducting Lutheran worship services in Waubay, South Dakota. Pastor Heinrich Ehlen came in 1892 and early that year a constitution was adopted. On Easter Sunday, April 17, an organization was effected with the name "Zion Congregation." In the spring of 1893 plans were made to build a house of worship. On July 9th a neat frame church could be dedicated to the service of the triune God. Zion was the first church erected in Waubay.

By 1925 the congregation had grown to such an extent that the original house of worship became too small. First plans were to build on to the old church but no real savings could be seen when comparing extensive additions to a completely new building. And so in January of 1925 a meeting was held and the decision was made to pattern a new church building after its sister church in Britton. On the day after Pentecost, Henry Holzerland came with his horses and broke the ground for the foundation of the new church which was erected a short distance east of the old one. The approximate cost of the new structure was $7,670 with members of the congregation helping as much as possible. The building was dedicated on November 22, 1925. That building still stands today as an important landmark in the northwest part of Waubay on a hill overlooking the town.

Numerous pastors have served faithfully at Zion. Pastor Larry Johnson has served since 1980.

Trinity Lutheran Church, Fairfax, South Dakota

The early history of Trinity Lutheran Church of Fairfax goes back to the 1890's when the Yankton Indian Agency at Greenwood was the headquarters of the Lutheran Movement. A call was issued to the Missouri Synod for a pastoral candidate.

In 1891 Candidate C.F.W. Walther, the "Ferdinand Walther," was assigned to this field. He came to Greenwood, South Dakota which was the port of landing for steamships on the Missouri River. He was the son of John Walther and grandson of Otto Herman Walther who was the brother of the famous C.F.W. Walther.

Pastor Walther lived in a sod house built for him at Poor Man's Bottom (now Sunshine Bottom) a few miles northeast of Lynch, Nebraska.

In 1894 Pastor W.F. G. Schneider came to Napier, Nebraska and relieved Walther of duties in the western end of this field. Pastor Schneider then preached at Fairfax and Bonesteel.

The Trinity Lutheran Church of Fairfax was organized in 1892 by Pastor Walther. Lutherans met in homes in the area for "Lutheran School" as well as worship conducted by laymen living in this area. The first church was erected about 1899 by the homesteading pioneers.

It is interesting to note that the Reverend A.C. Oesch served the longest tenure from 1932 to 1946 in Fairfax, as well as serving a ten-year vacancy at Spencer, Nebraska. He led his people through the Dirty Thirties and World War II. He sustained his body and soul by keeping a dairy herd and providing milk for much of the town.

Today Trinity is a dual parish with St. John's of Wagner.

St. John's Lutheran Church, Britton, South Dakota

The Federal Government Homestead Act of 1862 brought many settlers from Germany to Dakota Territory. A person who would occupy 160 acres of Government land for five years and pay a small fee would be able to claim the land as his own. In 1884 a city was platted and named Britton after Colonel Isaac Britton, an early resident. Many Lutherans were among the early settlers of this community.

Realizing their spiritual needs, in the spring of 1889 friends gathered to study the Scriptures. They realized their need for a pastor to lead them and found Reverend Ehlen who agreed to visit them when possible. Services were held at least once a month in various homes.

After three years God answered their prayers with the arrival of Pastor John Matzat. On October 30, 1892 the formal organization of "The German Evangelical Lutheran Saint John's Congregation U.A.C. (Unaltered Augsburg Confession)" was named. This name was incorporated one month later on November 5, 1892. They immediately decided on building a new house of worship.

It was in 1917 that the present church was built and dedicated to the glory of God for the worship of the people of Saint John's. The entire building (including furnishings) amounted to $9,000.

In 1928 the church's constitution was revised and translated into the English language.

In 1975 the front of the church was expanded to include a secretary's office and a library, a pastor's office and an extension of the narthex, and additional Sunday School rooms were added in the basement. In 1991 a fellowship hall and new kitchen were extended to the east.

St. John's Lutheran Church, Groton, South Dakota

The organization of Evangelical Lutheran St. John's Congregation took place on March 5, 1893. The first Lutheran services were held in Groton by Pastor Hinck followed some years later by Pastor C.C. Metz. It had been members from the James congregation west of Groton which came to organize St. John's.

On April 10, 1893 a special meeting was held at which a committee was authorized to buy the "college chapel" being offered for sale. The lot which is the present location of the church was also purchased. The chapel was then moved to that lot. The location of the church has not changed in these over 100 years!

In June 1908 it was decided to purchase 20 English hymnals and in July 1910 it was decided to have English services occasionally. In January of 1919 the decision was made that "January through April there would be alternate German and English services." The Ladies Aid was organized in 1910 and has remained active over the years.

The last voters' meeting minutes written in German were on April 29, 1928. Sunday services were alternated in language and in January 1929 it was directed that the "Midweek Lenten Service be in the same language as the preceding Sunday." In November, 1936 the voters decided that there would be English services each Sunday and German services one hour before on two Sundays each month. Diminishing attendance at the German language services soon brought about the complete elimination of them.

In 1931 the American Legion wanted to begin its youth baseball program in Groton. Several of the boys from St. John's were interested in being part of the program. A coach was needed. Pastor Wilke, a sports fan, volunteered to be the coach of the first American Legion Baseball team organized in Groton. Pastor Wilke's action made it possible for the Groton Legion Post to begin an on-going youth activity in which the youth of Groton have participated for many years. The first legion baseball was held in South Dakota in 1925.

It was apparent that the congregation needed a new church building. The last service held in the original church building was July 16, 1950, in which candidate Russell M. Grundmeier was ordained and installed as pastor of the congregation. The present church, with parish hall and kitchen, was built during 1950 and 1951. The church and new furnishings were dedicated to the Lord on November 25, 1951.

The symbols of the windows in the church – especially on the south side – convey the message of the Christian life beginning at the front with the symbol of Holy Baptism, then the hand of God the Father, then the Lamb of God, our Savior, Jesus Christ, then the dove (the symbol of the Holy Spirit), then the Holy Bible (open for us to study and believe), then the chalice and wafer (the symbols of Holy Communion), and lastly, the cross and crown (the symbols of the crown of life). The message – having been baptized in the name of God the Father, God the Son and God the Holy Spirit and continuing in His word and the sacrament of His body and blood, we shall receive the crown of life. These windows were purchased with funds given for this specific purpose. The preservation of these symbolic windows was a concern in the planning of the educational unit which was added to the building and dedicated in 1963. The courtyard between the two buildings was the answer to this concern. It allowed the sun to continue to light the symbolic windows as well as the adjacent windows of the education unit.

St. John's continued to grow under God's blessing. The Trinity, James, congregation disbanded on April 11, 1955 with a number of these members joining St. John's. St. John's assumed the responsibility of caring for the James cemetery four miles west of Groton.

St. John's Lutheran Church of West Hanson also held its last service on January 26, 1969. Many of these members joined St. John's congregation as well.

Since 1984 St. John's has taped its church services on Sunday mornings for showing on local cable TV with the cost covered by special individual contributions. These services not only are done for homebound members of St. John's but for the community at large as well.

An interesting note in the early history of St. John's states that

> *"the minutes of the early years of our congregation reveal that the treasurer was to list the members and to collect from each the amount that was his share of the cost. (The members were also reminded that each was to furnish two sacks of oats for the pastor's horses). The treasurer's subscription list gave way to the envelope system in the 1930's."*

The following history was sent to us by Dorene Nelson of St. John's in Groton:

> *"Reverend R.M. Grundmeier served as the pastor of St. John's Lutheran Church, Groton, South Dakota, for nearly 10 years from July 1950 to January 1960. He arrived in Groton as a single man, but during his time here he met and married the high school home economics teacher. The convenient location of the high school right across the street to the north of the church might have been conducive to the start of this lasting relationship. At their wedding, some of the men in the church jacked up Pastor's car so that the wheels were a few inches from the ground without it being obvious. The pastor and his new wife later attempted to leave on their honeymoon. They went nowhere!! Then a few of the now laughing congregational members gave the car a gentle push, and the happy couple was off. Many years later when Pastor Grundmeier retired from the ministry some representatives from the Groton congregation traveled to Sioux Falls to celebrate the occasion with the Grundmeier's. As a reminder of the car-jacking, they presented pastor with a cardboard cutout of a car. All of them enjoyed a good laugh over the memory."*

Through the strong preaching of the Word by faithful pastors over the years St. John's has remained a strong congregation firmly grounded in God's word.

Zion Lutheran Church, Avon, South Dakota

It was in the early 80's (perhaps 1881 or 1882) that Lutheran services were first conducted in Bon Homme County. Services were often held in homes – sod homes. Pastor Eichoff from the Kaylor-Scotland area served many of these people for a salary of $150 a year.

On February 28, 1889 five acres of land were bought for the sum of $20 from Dick Harbert and his wife. The same year the church was built four miles southeast of Avon at a cost of $418.35. All labor was donated by the members. This church was dedicated to the Triune God on September of 1889.

Shortly after the dedication of the new church, Reverend J.D. Ehlen was called to Kaylor and also served the Avon congregation until March 13, 1898.

In the year 1893 Zion congregation was incorporated according to the laws of the state of South Dakota. First resident pastor to serve was Pastor H.F. Lange, who served this parish until 1902.

In September 1902 Pastor Hermann Amend was called by the Avon congregation and served until 1909. During Pastor Amend's pastorate, services were also started and continued in the city of Avon, where a small church was built – total cost $491.40.

On September 12, 1909 Pastor G.W. Steinmeier was called. The congregation southeast of Avon decided to unite with the group in Avon. Immediately the parsonage was moved into town and the church building in the country was sold. Pastor Steinmeier served until November 1926.

In 1927 membership had increased to the extent that the old church could not accommodate the members. So a movement was started to build a larger church. Within a few months the building of a new church was in progress. The cost was $22,000.

On April 7, 1929 the beautiful church was dedicated to the service of the Triune God by a joyful and grateful congregation.

St. Paul's Lutheran Church, Delmont, South Dakota

St. Paul's Lutheran Church of Delmont dates back to the year 1896 when a group of homesteaders gathered at the home of Immanuel Hahn, Sr. This group attended worship services each Sunday at Immanuel Hahn's home. These services were led by a Pastor Kleinlein who suggested that the congregation name itself after the great Apostle Paul. Hence St. Paul's congregation was organized. In the Fall of 1897, Pastor J.D. Ehlen of Scotland served as Pastor.

Life was not easy on the prairie for these people. However their Christian faith, life and worship was important to them and to their children so they sacrificed greatly in order to have a congregation where they might worship and learn more about their great God and His plan of salvation.

On July 28, 1900 Pastor A.W. Kraft, a student of Concordia College of Springfield, Illinois was installed as the first resident pastor. He was ordained in the living room of Immanuel Hahn's house and lived in a remodeled grainery on the Hahn homestead. It was Pastor Kraft who helped organize the Christian Day School, which continued until 1927. He served St. Paul's until 1910 when he accepted a call to Yale, South Dakota. Various pastors then served following Pastor Kraft. St. Paul's congregation purchased 5 acres of ground in 1901 for the price of $55. St. Paul's then purchased the church building from the Delmont Town Congregation and placed it on dollies and pulled it with tractors to the present church site. The church was dedicated to the honor and glory of God on August 2, 1914 and was known as St. Paul's German Lutheran Church. St. Paul's congregation was disbanded on January 22, 2004. Only eternity will tell the number of souls that were touched by the message of the Gospel proclaimed at St. Paul's!

St. John's Lutheran Church, Wagner, South Dakota

"The mid to late 1800's found homesteads, immigrants, and expanding railroads followed by incorporated towns, except on the Yankton Sioux Reservation. By 1858 the Reservation had dwindled to 433,000 acres of eastern Charles Mix County. Compared to neighboring counties, development and changes in Charles Mix County would wait for 37 years. 1858 saw the birth of the agency town of Greenwood. The years 1869 and 1870 brought the arrival of two white missionaries. About the same time, a few fur traders settled along the Missouri River. Fur trader Fred Burn's daughter, Helen (Hennies), became an active long time St. John member.

"Fort Randall lay about 13 miles upstream from Greenwood and across the Missouri River. In 1893 the Army closed and abandoned the Fort. Thus, a Springfield stagecoach ended its service to the area. By 1895 the fleet of steamboats that sailed the length of the Missouri River had dwindled to one. Soon afterwards this boat was sold.

"President Cleveland made a proclamation in May of 1895 to open Charles Mix County to homesteaders. The sale of surplus land and homesteads brought charter members of St. John's Lutheran to the Wagner area." *(Taken from history of St. John's)*

The first worship service of what was later to become St. John's Lutheran, was held at the Henry Evers homestead home on Easter Sunday 1898. The Reverend H. Lange, pastor of Zion Lutheran Church in Avon conducted the service.

On June 14,1899, fifty two years after the Lutheran Church – Missouri Synod was organized, the charter for St. John's Lutheran Church was signed.

In 1900, Pastor Albert Kraft of St. Paul's, Delmont was given permission by his congregation to become a Circuit Rider minister. As part of his ministry, he held worship services in a schoolhouse south of the village of Wagner. During this time he also served Platte, and later, Geddes. He served these parishes by horse and buggy.

St. John's Evangelical Lutheran Church bought two lots in southeast Wagner at 3rd and Sheridan on June 17, 1907. The church built on the north lot was the congregation's first building and would be used for the next 40 years.

About 1920-21 Pastor Gade became the first pastor who served St. John's that had the use of an automobile. The slow, but reliable horses and buggy were kept for several years just in case they were needed.

Starting about 1926, Pastor Gade conducted a Sunday afternoon church service at Ree #5 School, 12 1/2 miles south of today's Wagner community school. For a time in 1927 services were held in a vacant house nine miles south of Wagner on the Cemetery Road and 3/4 miles west. At this house, William Uecker was baptized as an adult. As time continued on, the Third and Sheridan church was becoming crowded, and so building plans were in progress for a new church. In April 1945, Carl and Amanda Rehwaldt bought and presented the lots to St. John's Lutheran Congregation. Ground was broken in June of 1947 for the new structure. The ceremony for the cornerstone laying was Sunday, November 2, 1947. On June 19, 1949 a new church was dedicated in conjunction with St. John's 50th anniversary.

An addition was built onto the church in 1984-1985 in order to eliminate the icy outside church steps and provide for more room in the church basement.

Pastor Clark Gies, (retired pastor living in South Dakota) served as pastor of St. John's from 1966 until 2003.

Emanuel Lutheran Church, Sisseton, South Dakota

In the year 1892 the Sisseton-Wahpeton Indian Reservation was open for settlement and, within the period of the following three years, a large number of German-speaking families had purchased homestead rights and established homes in the Sisseton area. Circuit ministers would come by horse and buggy or wagon when time and weather permitted them to serve these scattered Lutherans.

The first pastor to be called to serve was Pastor Eifert who lived at Wilmot. On July 30, 1899 plans were made for the first house of worship. The first church was also to serve as a public school for the community children. In 1902 the congregation accepted a gift of land to be used as the future site of the church as well as a church cemetery. Pastor Huesner became the first resident pastor in 1903.

In 1913 Pastor Steffen came. He conducted a parochial school with a full elementary schedule for the community. Under his guidance, the present church was built in the spring of 1916. Pastor Steffen was the first pastor to use the "gas buggie."

In 1948 much discussion was held about the possibility of moving the church into town. The result was that both the church and the parsonage were moved. The letters on the cornerstone were changed to English and the laying of the stone took place in September of 1948. Pastor Vogel, pastor at that time, spent much time evaluating conditions of South Dakota Indians and trying to determine whether the congregation should continue to increase evangelism efforts among them.

It was in 1998 that Emanuel celebrated its 100th anniversary. Through God's grace, Emanuel continues to grow in faith and hopes to celebrate His mercy and love for years to come.

St. Paul's Lutheran Church, Ferney, South Dakota

As early as 1880 the spiritual needs of the predominantly Lutheran community of Ferney were met in a mission station located in the Fred Schmidt School located two miles north and four miles east of Ferney. Reverend Pfotenhauer, who later became President of the Lutheran Church – Missouri Synod, was one of the early missionaries to serve in this area. Another missionary was F.W. Wenger, who later became a professor at Concordia Seminary in Springfield. It was on October 14, 1900 that a group of Lutherans met at the Ferney School for the purpose of organizing as a congregation. A constitution was written, adopted and signed by ten people.

On May 27, 1901 the Articles of Incorporation were filed with the name, "German Evangelical Lutheran St. John's Church of Ferney." At this time Voters' meetings were held once a year.

In 1902 the mission station at the Schmidt school was discontinued, with some of the members joining the Ferney church and the rest going to Andover.

The West Hanson Lutheran Church was the first Lutheran church built in this area. The congregations of Ferney and West Hanson were served during this time by Pastor Haertling. He came from Aberdeen one or two days a month.

It was in 1904 that the Ferney members decided to build a church. Construction was started and the church was completed in the spring of 1905 at the cost of $2,000. The members donated much of the labor.

In 1923 the Voters decided to assess each member $5 a year and do away with Sunday collections for the home church.

A ladies aid and Sunday School were organized in 1926. Men sat in the left pews and women sat on the right side. Women were expected, but not required, to wear a hat or scarf on their heads.

In 1927 a revised constitution was adopted and the name was changed from St. John's to St. Paul's Lutheran. Later that year, St. Paul's became an official member of the Lutheran Church – Missouri Synod.

In 1935, after Pastor Dommer accepted a call, Pastor Frank Wilke of Groton served as vacancy pastor. Ferney and Groton became one parish served by Pastor Wilke. In 1949 the Ferney congregation left Groton and joined with the Andover congregation as a parish.

The need for a new church became apparent. On June 17, 1961 a groundbreaking ceremony was held and building plans began to progress. The estimated cost was $85,000. On September 8, 1963 the new church was dedicated.

In 1969 St. John's of West Hanson held its last service. Some of the members joined St. Paul's of Ferney while others joined neighboring congregations.

Zion Lutheran Church, Delmont, South Dakota

In the year 1900, Reverend C.J. Messerli, pastor of Zion Lutheran Church, which was located 4 miles northwest of Delmont started a church in the town of Delmont. They formed a constitution and called the new church the Evangelical Lutheran Emanuels Congregation U.A.C.

The new church built in 1901 was dedicated by Dr. J.F. Pfotenhauer who became President of the Lutheran Church – Missouri Synod in 1911. In 1902 the members of the rural congregation, Zion, and the town congregation, Emmanuel decided to unite and

Zion Lutheran Church, Delmont, SD

form one church. It was decided to have a church in town but use the name of the country church, Zion. In April 1902 the newly called Pastor, Reverend Christian Wieting, was installed. The congregation numbered 227 souls with forty-seven children in the parochial school. In 1907 the present church yard was purchased and in 1908 the church building was moved across the street to the present location. In 1912 it became evident that more room was needed and so it was decided to build a new church.

Today Zion Lutheran Church forms a parish with Emmaus Lutheran Church of Tripp, South Dakota.

Chapter 9
1900-1920

St. Paul's Lutheran Church, Seneca, South Dakota

Lutherans were known to live in the Seneca area back as early as 1890 and before.

In the early 1900's the Seneca area was served by a Circuit Rider Minister from Orient. Shortly thereafter, church was held in the Methodist church with Reverend William Dommer as pastor.

About 1915 the school house in Seneca was rented, making it possible to have Sunday morning worship services, which improved attendance greatly.

In 1926 the present church was built by the congregation with labor being donated. The total cash outlay for the building was $2,600.

The church was dedicated on September 26, 1926 with the sermon being delivered by Reverend Dommer of Andover, South Dakota, former pastor.

The minister's salary in 1936 was $23 per month. His total salary for the year was $900, plus his home in Lebanon. This same year communion was changed from four times a year to once a month.

In 1946, Seneca joined the Lutheran Church – Missouri Synod.

In 1974 Seneca and Lebanon divided.

It was in 1982 that Seneca began to be served by the Gettysburg and Lebanon churches.

Emmaus Lutheran Church, Tripp, South Dakota

In 1870 many of the German people living in Southern Russia decided to leave and go to America. They had lost many of their freedoms, especially their religious freedom, and so a new life was sought. These people came from many areas in Southern Russia; from the town of Odessa and Teplitz, as well as the regions of Bessarbia, Crimea and along the Volga River area. They arrived in New York City after 14 days at sea and in five more days they reached Yankton, Dakota Territory which was the terminal of the railroad at that time. From Yankton they headed west and north with their families to find a land on which to settle. A place to worship was one of their first concerns.

In 1874 Missionary Reverend Doescher, a Missouri Synod pastor, came from Fort Dodge, Iowa and settled in Yankton. He visited many of the settlements springing up in this area. One of the first churches built was in Odessa, southeast of Scotland.

"The Traveling Preacher" - Emmaus, Tripp

Services at this time were held in homes until church buildings were built. In some cases schools and parsonages were also built. It was during the pastorate of Reverend J.D. Ehlen (pastor of St. John's in Kaylor, the mother church from 1890 to 1920) that Emmaus was organized. The date of organization was April 4, 1901.

Emmaus' first building was moved in from the country and placed on a lot south of the present building. The steeple and chancel were added and the building was dedicated on May 12, 1901.

As the membership continued to increase, a new building was needed. On August 31, 1913 a new building was dedicated. The old church was sold for $225 and moved away.

There was a two month vacancy after Pastor Gerike left Emmaus and Pastor John Dewald was installed in November of 1928. It was during his ministry that Zion congregation southwest of Tripp decided to close and join with the Emmaus congregation. The last service at Zion was March 13, 1938. In the mid 1990's one of the members gave a substantial monetary gift for the improvement of the church building and for mission work. Thankful for the gift, the congregation decided to close the basement of the church and added a parish hall to the south. A new entrance was added to the church building.

By the end of 1995 the project was completed and dedication was held on February 18, 1996. Eberlein Hall is used today for many gatherings and meetings for the church.

St. Paul's Lutheran Church, Scotland, South Dakota

The beginning of St. Paul's Lutheran Church goes back to the days when Pastor J.D. Ehlen was residing some 7 miles northwest of Scotland, serving St. John's Lutheran Church and also preaching and organizing Lutheran congregations in the surrounding towns. Pastor Ehlen began preaching in the town of Scotland in the year 1900.

Early statistical yearbooks list Scotland as a preaching station in 1900. No organized congregation existed as of this time. However in 1901 the yearbook does list statistics and so, although the exact date is unknown, it is evident that the actual organization of St. Paul's Lutheran Church took place somewhere in the early part of 1901.

The first three resident pastors served this parish for a period of 50 years. While Pastor Ehlen served, he also served the church at large as Synodical Visitor, member of the Mission Board, Vice-President and as District President from 1912 to 1918. He served this parish for 30 years. Both he and his wife are buried in the Scotland cemetery. It soon became evident that the original church building acquired in 1901 was not suitable to accommodate the congregation. And so on October 1, 1944 the voting members of St. Paul's decided to start a building fund. On October 5, 1947 a church plan prepared by Mr. Karl Neumeister (a member of St. Paul's) was accepted and work continued in gathering the necessary funds. The old building was disposed of in July of 1950 and a groundbreaking ceremony was held July 23rd. Building plans were begun shortly thereafter. This church structure serves wonderfully the needs of the people in this area, proclaiming the message of the gospel of Jesus Christ.

Zion Lutheran Church, Andover, South Dakota

In 1892 a number of Lutherans of German descent met in a schoolhouse between Andover and Ferney, SD and decided to ask Reverend H. Ehlen of Hanson Township to serve them as often as possible. These families pledged their attendance and support. (Wouldn't it be nice today if our members also pledged their support to be there when the pastor proclaimed the Word??? – we do make that promise to our pastors in their Call documents). These

German Lutheran pioneers stayed with their arrangement, meeting in the Schmidt School for some ten years. Many a trip was made to that little house of worship in a sled drawn by oxen. Often snow had to be scooped out of the building before services could begin. Despite these problems, their love for God's word only increased and attendance was almost always perfect to those who had agreed to be there. Articles of Incorporation were signed in 1902.

In 1903 those living in Day County felt that they were numerous enough to have services nearer their home. Thus, they started services in rented buildings in Andover. Pastors from Groton served this group of faithful Lutherans.

In 1908 the congregation decided to erect a framed church building in town. As the years passed more Lutherans from other states settled in this vicinity and joined the congregation. As the congregation maintained its own ministry, it became self-sustaining and in May of 1920 was released from Groton and proceeded to call a minister of its own. The Reverend F.W.F. Dommer, Lebanon, SD was called and became the first resident pastor of this congregation. Pastor Dommer served until 1935, when he accepted a call to Missouri. Pastor Frank E. Wilke of Groton was asked to serve as vacancy pastor. In 1936 Candidate Erwin Boeschen was installed as pastor of the Andover congregation. He served Zion congregation until 1941, when Reverend Lester A. Oberheu of Rockham, SD was called and installed as pastor.

In 1943 the congregation purchased at public auction from the county, land in the city of Andover, which would be the home of their new church building.

In 1950 Pastor J.E. Schwarting of Groton accepted the call to Zion and was installed on New Year's Day 1950. Various pastors served since that time.

During the spring of 1961, the congregation resolved to build a new house of worship. This was begun in August of 1961 and completed by the first week of February 1962. God's continued blessings dwell daily among His chosen ones at Andover to this day.

St. John's Lutheran Church, Gregory, South Dakota

In the summer of 1905 Pastor Weertz and Pastor R. Krenzien from Nebraska made trips into the newly opened Rosebud territory. They found a number of Lutheran families around Gregory and South Dallas. Immediately, services were held in the home of Fred Knittel, who was living about 6 miles south of Dallas, South Dakota. Soon thereafter services were also held in Gregory, in the back of the saloon of Jacob Reider. Services were held quite irregularly until a Candidate was called and arrived to serve these

Lutheran Christians.

When Candidate Burandt arrived in August of 1905 he was given lodging in the Reider Tavern until the city of Gregory gave each congregation in the city a 1/2 block of ground. Here the congregation quickly erected a house for its pastor.

About the same time that the house was erected the congregation moved its place of worship to the site of the old Gregory Theater. Following this they moved to the Odd Fellows Hall, which was an upstairs room at the southeast corner of 5th and Main. Candidate Burandt had arrived with team and buggy as his means of travel. From the Gregory area he served also the West Carlock congregation known as the former South Dallas congregation.

The congregation in Gregory then built its church in the months of June and July of 1907 and were moved in by July of the same year following completion of the church building. The congregation also built a barn for the pastor's horses.

Congregation at St. John's Lutheran Church, Gregory in new church

But now God was sending them a new pastor who was married and had a child. Thus another bedroom needed to be added to this two-room house. His term of service was short, as God had different plans for him. His health continued to fail until he could no longer serve the congregation. They then called the Reverend John Dewald. Reverend Dewald received $135 per year from the Gregory congregation. From historical information, it seems that a like sum was matched by the Mission Board and from the South Dallas congregation which Pastor Dewald also served. Pastor Dewald was single when he arrived, but took a bride one year after he was at Gregory. He was also the first pastor to have a car. This car was purchased for him by the congregation in about 1917 and remained the property of the congregation.

Some of the congregational minutes from 1920 indicated that a motion was made to have English dropped from the services. However this motion did not carry.

In 1928 a Pastor Weinhold came to Schneider, NE. Prior to his leaving Gregory for Schneider, he was serving 6 congregations, namely: Carlock, Dixon, Lucas, South Dallas, Dallas and Gregory. Note: Now our three point parishes (of which we still have a few) don't seem impossible after all.

On April 9, 1928, the congregations of Dallas and West Carlock, in regular meeting, decided to call a pastor of their own. In the early 1930's, this part of the country went through some trying years. Even though 1932 had shown a fair crop, its monetary value was worthless. So the congregation was forced to ask for assistance from the Mission Board. There were no farm programs at that time to aid farmers who had lost crops. This financial assistance was necessary throughout Reverend Dewald's pastorate due to the fact that dust and grasshoppers, in succeeding years, granted little subsistence from the land. However, by God's grace this congregation continued. Even though Pastor Dewald had a family of six, God continued to provide for them as they served the people of God in Gregory and the surrounding communities. In February of 1950, the Zion congregation of South Dallas agreed to discontinue services and attend services in another Lutheran church of the synodical conference. This lightened the pastor's load to be able to continue to serve. However, it also posed another big problem. The Gregory church to which many of the members came, and which had faithfully served since 1907 would not be large enough for the increase (what a wonderful problem). So the slightly larger Legion Hall in town was put to the congregation's use. However it seemed that a new building would be the best answer to their problems and so, July 10 and 11, 1950, the old building was torn down and a resolution to build a new church was adopted. The basement was dug, the walls were going up, steel joists were placed into position and finishing work was begun. Finally, the basement was ready for services on Christmas Eve of 1950. Almost 200 people crowded into the basement for that first service. From this basement building, then a building of stone, wood and steel would be put on top to serve as the edifice of the new church. Much of the time and labor was spent by members of the congregation in making this dream come true. A loan from Church Extension Fund of the South Dakota District made the completion of their church possible. This building was dedicated on December 13, 1953. In praise and thanksgiving for this wonderful house of worship the first service held was a mission festival to praise God as well as to reach out to others with the saving Gospel of Jesus Christ. Over 300 people attended this service.

In January of 1956, Saint Paul's congregation of Dallas decided to disband and most of its members joined the congregation at Gregory.

Various pastors faithfully served these Christian people since that time. A note in their history says, "...*a history of the congregation could well be called 'a book of Acts' of that congregation. Much of the history is found in the sacred acts performed over the years. These acts are a record of joys and of tears, of struggles and of growth.*"

Their records also indicate that if a record could be kept of the many times that the Gospel had been preached from the pulpit or the Grace of God dispensed in the Lord's Supper, this would be voluminous because God's Grace was there ever present in the Word and Sacraments and was finally recorded when God's faithful people were gathered to the Church Triumphant. *"A living record is found in the hearts and lives of those who are the members of this congregation. It is a history of joy, hope and love. This volume cannot be written, for it would fill endless volumes. It can be read in the life and testimony of each member, past and present, of the congregation."*

And thus God continues to bless this congregation as He does all of the congregations of our beloved South Dakota District until He finally gathers His people to the Church Triumphant where the hardships and sorrows will all be left behind.

Christ Lutheran Church, Lebanon, South Dakota

It was on September 25, 1906 that Christ Lutheran Church of Lebanon, South Dakota was organized under the leadership of the Reverend August Sauer. At this same meeting of organization they adopted the name of Christ Lutheran Church. The Constitution of the congregation was adopted on October 30, 1907. At that time the parish consisted of three congregations, namely: Agar, Lebanon and Pembroke. Agar and Lebanon are still functioning today. Later Seneca and Gettysburg were added to this parish. In 1928 the parish split with Lebanon, Pembroke and Seneca forming one parish and Gettysburg and Agar forming a second parish. In 1955 Pembroke left this parish and joined Gettysburg. Soon the Pembroke congregation closed. Lebanon and Seneca worshiped as a joint parish until 1974, when Lebanon joined the Gettysburg parish. A church was built for the members of Christ Lutheran congregation and dedicated in September of 1925. Pastor F.A. Hinners was serving the congregation at this time. Various pastors served Christ over the course of these past years. Pastor H.W. Augustin was the last resident pastor who served Christ congregation. Following his departure, Lebanon joined with Gettysburg to form a new parish under the direction of Pastor Robert E. Utecht. Lebanon is still joined with Gettysburg as a parish today, which also serves the congregation at Seneca.

St. Peter Lutheran Church, Midland, South Dakota

In the year 1905 the first families began to file homestead rights in the area north of Stamford, SD. The railroad at this time came as far west as Presho, but in 1906 it continued on westward to Belvidere and brought even more homesteaders to this area.

Early in 1907 Reverend Gade of White Lake received word that many Lutherans had come to the area north of Stamford and so he came by train to check into this. When he found this to be true he held the first worship service at the home of Mrs. Christina Rothenberger.

In the spring of 1907 the St. Peter Evangelical Lutheran Church of rural Midland was organized. The land was do-

High on a hill stands St. Peter Lutheran Church, rural Midland, SD

nated by Peter Rothenberger for the church and the members immediately began to build their own house of worship. This church was dedicated on July 21, 1907. Candidate Theodore Kissling was ordained and installed as pastor the same day. In 1907 the congregation was received into membership with the Evangelical Lutheran Synod of Missouri, Ohio and other states.

From 1908 to 1917 St. Peter congregation maintained a parochial school taught by the pastor. However, the school was discontinued during World War I because of factions outside the church. German services were held at St. Peter until the mid 1940's.

The original church building housed the congregation until the fall of 1946, when ground was broken for a new church building. The basement served as a house of worship until 1950 when the new church was completed. It was built almost entirely out of cedar, 4x4 tongue in groove, nailed together with 60 penny spikes. Almost all of the work was done by members of the church with two carpenters supervising.

On October 1, 1950 the congregation dedicated its new building and installed and ordained its new pastor, the Reverend Alva F. Pingel.

For most of the years between 1907 and 1967 the St. Peter congregation formed a dual parish with Zion Lutheran Church of Kadoka.

In the 1950's the church building was destroyed by fire and during a severe thunderstorm early Friday morning, July 2, 1976 it was again destroyed by lightning. The fire was not discovered until it was too late to save anything. All the records which were housed in the basement were destroyed.

On Sunday morning, July 4, 1976 the congregation met in the home of Lloyd Reiman for a Communion Service as well as to give praise and thanks to our gracious God for preserving our country and its freedoms for 200 years. In a special meeting the next day, July 5, 1976 the congregation voted unanimously to rebuild on the same location. Late that summer the congregation decided to buy the old Immaculate Conception Church at Bonesteel, South Dakota for the sum of $5,000. This was then moved to the site on the hill where the new basement had been dug. The church was struck by lightning during the move to its destination. On May 2, of 1978 this new building was set on the basement and on March 4, 1979 the first service was held in this remodeled building. It was dedicated on June 3, 1979 to the glory of God for the worship of His people.

On March 7, 1993 St. Peter became a dual parish with St. John of Norris. St. Peter Lutheran Church is the oldest Missouri Synod congregation in western South Dakota. St. Peter has been served by various pastors and lay ministers over these almost 100 years.

If you travel east of Kadoka and look north on one of the high hills three miles north from the area of the Old Town you'll see St. Peter Lutheran standing high as its steeple points heavenward to the God which it serves.

St. John's Lutheran Church, Chester, South Dakota

It was back in 1902 that a group of Lutheran families in the area of Chester asked the Reverend Oberheu of Wentworth, SD to come and serve them. Worship services were thus held in various homes and a country school house.

On May 19, 1907 St. John's Lutheran congregation was formally organized. The first church was built and dedicated on December 22, 1907. The Reverend Paul Schornack, the first pastor was installed on July 19, 1914. The present church was built and dedicated in 1949 with a new addition being added and dedicated in 1975.

St. John's provided a number of young men who have or are now serving as pastors in the ministry of the Lutheran Church – Missouri Synod. They are: Professor J. Henry Gienapp; Dr. Norman Gienapp; Reverend Arthur Schornack; and Reverend Richard Dannenbring. Augusta Gienapp, Gretchen

Gienapp-Beecroft and Melanie Schuldt-Maddick also served the church in our parochial schools.

In 1940 St. John's congregation became a member of the Lutheran Church – Missouri Synod.

It was in 1962 that St. John's officially formed a dual parish with St. Peter's Lutheran Church of Wentworth – an arrangement which is still in existence today.

Zion Lutheran Church, Hoven (Pembroke), South Dakota

Zion Lutheran Church of Pembroke, SD was organized on March 14, 1909. Soon after, it became a member of the Lutheran Church – Missouri Synod.

On March 28, 1928 a joint meeting was held where it was decided that the congregations at Gettysburg and Agar would join and form a parish and Pembroke, Lebanon and Seneca would join to form a parish.

It is interesting to note that, in the history of this congregation, it decided in 1936 to farm 80 acres, of which the proceeds would be used for church debts. This arrangement for farming this land was discontinued in 1938.

In December of 1944 it was decided that Pembroke would join with Gettysburg and Agar to form a parish.

In March of 1948 Pastor O.D. Brack was installed as pastor of this parish (Pastor Brack still serves our District as Hospital Chaplain in Sioux Falls).

In 1956 the congregation voted to disband temporarily and has been closed since that time.

St. Paul's Lutheran Church, Draper, South Dakota

Some time in the beginning of the 20th century, when land west of the Missouri River was open for homesteading, a number of Lutheran families were included in the rush of settlers who eagerly sought new homes in this vast land. They soon acknowledged the need for guidance from the Almighty, and, remembering the teaching of their forefathers, they began holding worship meetings. Whenever possible, circuit riding pastors conducted services which were held in private homes.

The Draper Lutherans were a part of a mission field which included Brule, Lyman, and Stanley counties. Pastor Fred Gade was the first to serve this region in 1907. He would make missionary journeys through Lyman and Stanley counties from his parish at White Lake. In 1908, Reverend Theodore Kissling was assigned to this field. He lived in Stamford and served both the Draper and Murdo areas until 1909, when Reverend Gustav Steffan took over the work in this field.

St. Paul's congregation was organized in 1909 and in 1912 had the church building moved to the land about 10 miles north of Draper.

The depression years were hard on the population of this area. Many of the settlers found it difficult to make a living. Grasshoppers were eating up crops, and drought, along with brutally severe winters took their toll, causing many settlers to sell their homesteads and start anew somewhere else. Those remaining trusted in the Lord and continued to worship in the little white church for more than 30 years.

For many of the "horse and buggy" years the church was served by pastors from Presho or Stamford. In 1923 Draper joined with Murdo and formed a dual parish. It was at this time also that a group of Lutherans south of Draper began holding services at the town hall. It was often necessary to clean up the remains of a Saturday night dance before services could be held. During winter months it was not unusual to put a robe on over an overcoat, as the congregation sat huddled together as close to an old pot-bellied stove as they could get. The breath of the members was visible during the singing of the hymns, and matters were not helped by the fact that there were no windows in the building, but rather cloth tacked rather loosely over the space where the windows should have been. So it was with great joy that the first service was held in a new church.

In 1944 the congregation decided to build a church in the town of Draper. The building was completed and the cornerstone was laid on March 6, 1946. The building was dedicated to the glory of God and to the preaching of His Word on March 16, 1947.

Immanuel Lutheran Church, Harrold, South Dakota

On March 20, 1910 Immanuel Lutheran Church was organized by Rev. F. W. Leyhe, Pastor at Wolsey, South Dakota. The first services conducted by Pastor Leyhe were held in the Fred Winckler home. The first resident pastor was Pastor Dauten Hahn. The first church stood on the same location as the present church. During the years of 1910 to 1923 God blessed this congregation as it grew considerably in membership so that the old church building would no longer accommodate the numbers for Sunday morning worship. Thus it was on February 25, 1923 that a meeting was held to discuss the building of a new and larger church.

It was decided to sell the old church, (which was then moved to the west side of town and converted into a home), and to build a new church.

The following sons of the congregation served in the Office of the Holy Ministry over the past years: Luther Bauer, Floyd Gogolin, Wallace Misterek, Emil Winckler and Albert Winckler.

Immanuel at Harrold is known as the mother church in this area of our state. It is served by the Pastor from the Agar/Onida parish.

Zion Lutheran Church, Rapid City, SD

Founding a congregation in western South Dakota was not easy because the potential members were scattered on isolated farms and small towns. As early as 1889, German speaking pastors traveled through the area preaching and celebrating the sacraments, but not enough Lutherans inhabited the area to support a resident pastor. However, in 1910 the South Dakota District of the Lutheran Church – Missouri Synod decided that a pastor was needed to serve the scattered Lutherans. They asked the Synod for a seminary graduate and on August 21, 1910, Oscar Heilman held a service in Rapid City for 33 people. He not only served people in Rapid City but was expected to serve settlements in the entire area and on two out of every three Sundays he was out preaching in the community from Sturgis on the north to Wayside, NE, on the south. In 1912 Pastor Heilman accepted a call to Montana. It was then in 1913 that the South Dakota District again asked for a candidate from the seminary and the call was assigned to Walter Nitschke.

Now the congregation needed a place to worship. In the initial year, 1910, this small group obtained permission from the city to use City Hall. After the year was over the leaders rented the Methodist church and in 1916, after they had collected some money, they purchased three lots on the corner of 5th and Quincy for $1,100 and bought a former Baptist church which was being used as a school for $200. This building was moved from 7th and Columbus to 5th and Quincy where it was placed on a foundation and remodeled for use as their church. A cross was placed in the tower and a coat of paint was applied to the building. This building was later moved to the corner of 5th and St. Patrick and, several years ago, was devastated by fire. On May 18, 1916 the congregation asked the District for support to pay its pastor's salary. They also agreed to affiliate with the Lutheran Church – Missouri Synod. A Sunday School was started in 1921.

By 1941 Zion's membership was 236 and a single service could not accommodate all the members. In 1949 the voters authorized that an architect be engaged to draw up plans for a church costing $30,000. The next year they accepted a bid from a contractor for $46,420.

The last service in the old church was held on July 30, 1950 and the congregation transferred the worship services and Sunday School to the State Theatre. In February of 1951 the congregation returned to 5th and Quincy and held services in the basement and finally on April 29, 1951 the church was dedicated. It was spacious enough so that all the members could be accommodated in one service. The new building had a seating capacity of 400 in the nave. Within three years the congregation grew rapidly, increasing in membership so that a second morning service had to be established.

Early in 1955 the congregation contracted for the construction of an educational wing costing $81,046. The baby-boomers were reaching school-age, so the voters decided it was an opportune time to found a Christian Day School, a possibility that had been considered for some time. In 1957 Miss Anita Klepel began teaching 21 pupils in the first four grades.

In the years following, parking was needed as well as a playground for children and so the congregation began purchasing lots adjacent to its property at 5th and Quincy.

On June 9, 1972, a devastating flood hit the west and downtown areas of Rapid City which claimed the lives of some 238 people. Fifty-five families of Zion had suffered loss of some kind or another and needed help from the congregation. The parsonage also sustained much damage. By the mid 1980's Zion had reached a point where buildings were inadequate to meet the needs of the growing congregation. Many meetings were held to decide whether the best place was to rebuild on the present property or to seek new land for the structure of a church and school. Since properties around the present location were not for sale, in 1994 a site, suitable and scenic, was available on the east side of South Highway 16 on a ridge overlooking Rapid City. This 32-acre piece of ground was purchased from funds which had been collected over the years for this purpose. In June 1998, ground was broken and the construction firm Gustafson Builders began work on the 2.4 million dollar structure which was dedicated one year later.

Zion Rapid City was served by a number of pastors who later became Presidents of the South Dakota District, namely: Walter Nitschke, Paul Wendling and Raymond Hartwig. Pastor Phillip Mueller, who had served as District President years before, became Assistant to the Pastor in 1970.

Emmanuel Lutheran Church, Creighton, South Dakota

Immigrants of German ethnic origin from the Crimea were among the first settlers at Creighton. The Russian Czar was putting pressure on these people to relinquish some of their former political and religious liberties which they had enjoyed in the Crimea for about 100 years. This caused them to leave their beautiful and productive farms in the Crimea, a peninsula in the Black Sea and settle in Tripp, South Dakota. In 1907 most of this group homesteaded in the Creighton area.

Soon these homesteaders of the Lutheran faith realized their need for spiritual leadership and contacts were made with Missionary G. Hoelscher of Philip. Thus, from 1907 to 1909, services were held in their homes about once a month.

On January 7, 1910 at the home of Henry Hirsch, the Emmanuel congregation was organized. A site for the new church and cemetery was chosen. By September of 1910 the first house of worship was completed and on the first Sunday of the month, September 4, 1910, this building was dedicated by acting synodical President, Pastor Pfotenhauer. These services were conducted in the German language.

In spite of suffering, afflictions, and bearing crosses, they built a church of finished lumber while they themselves lived behind walls of sod and tar paper shanties.

As the church continued to grow, it was evident that more space was needed for worship services as well as Sunday School for the 45 children enrolled. A campaign was held to raise money for a building to serve the congregation. This new house of worship was built one mile north of Creighton along the main road through the community. October 6, 1957 marks the date where a groundbreaking ceremony was held and construction began. Much labor was donated by the men of the congregation to save on costs.

Bethesda Lutheran Church, Marion, South Dakota

Records on the early years of Bethesda Lutheran Church are quite scant. However from some of the records of St. Paul's Lutheran Church at Freeman it is shown that Pastor A. Mueller served the Lutheran people in and around Marion as early as 1880. The first baptism was on July 11, 1880 and the first marriage recorded is on June 3, 1881. The first confirmation class was confirmed in 1882. Pastor A.C. Oberheu of Parker and Wellington held the first public worship service on September 24, 1911.

On July 21, 1912 Bethesda was organized under the leadership of Pastor A. Sauer from Canistota. A church building was purchased from the Methodists and moved to the corner of Dakota and State Street which served as the house of worship for some 45 years. In 1947 a building was purchased from Bethesda Mennonite Community Church and was dedicated to the glory of God on November 17, 1957 under the leadership of Pastor P.R. Albrecht of Canistota. On April 1, 1915 the congregation joined the Lutheran Church – Missouri Synod. A Christian Day School was maintained from 1907 to 1923. Due to financial burdens the school was discontinued in 1923.

Bethesda is now a dual parish with First English Lutheran of Parker and is in the Freeman Circuit.

Zion Lutheran Church, Hamill, South Dakota

On Sunday, May 4, 1913 a Swedish worship service was called for the purpose of organizing a Swedish Evangelical Lutheran congregation. Scandinavian people living in and around Hamill came in order to accomplish this venture. The motion passed that the congregation's name would be Swedish Evangelical Zion Lutheran Congregation of Tripp County of South Dakota. The first pastor to serve the new congregation was the Reverend J.J. Richards. This congregation was planned and organized in 1911 and 1912.

On July 1, 1923 three lots were purchased by the Ladies Aid for $135. A parsonage was built at a total cost (including cistern) of $4,530. There was a large Sunday School, Ladies Aid and active Luther League. The Ladies Aid was spoken of as the financial backbone of the church for many years.

Prior to 1961 a building fund was started which could be used someday to enlarge and improve the church. On May 10, 1961 a drive was successfully made and the building committee made plans to expand. On May 20, the basement was dug, but due to heavy rains, it took longer to get the basement wall poured. By July 7th the church was jacked up and moved off its spot where it had been for so many years.

The first service in the new church was held on June 10, 1962 followed by dedication on June 17th.

When a vacancy in the pastoral office occurred, Pastor Richard Hardel of Christ Lutheran Church in Winner served the vacancy. During his pastorate, Zion made the decision to join the Lutheran Church – Missouri Synod which was the beginning of the Winner-Clearfield-Hamill tri-point parish. This congregation is still being served as a three-point parish with Winner and Clearfield.

Zion Lutheran Church, Wessington Springs, South Dakota

In the late 1800's, vast areas of the Dakota Territory remained unexplored, even though many people were moving into it. Pastor Andrew Mueller was called as a Missionary who lived in Marion and served Sioux Falls, Mitchell, Alexandria, Mount Vernon, Plankinton, etc. In 1883 he began serving Wessington Springs as well. Later, mission work in the Lutheran faith was begun in Wessington Springs by Reverend F. Israel, pastor of St. John's Lutheran Church – Missouri Synod of Lane, SD. This was about 1912. The first worship services were held in the Wessington Springs opera house and after a short time the Congregational Church was rented for services and Sunday School.

By the end of 1914 a constitution was adopted and the congregation became known as Zion Evangelical Lutheran Church. As suitable buildings were not available, it was decided to erect a new house of worship. Three lots were acquired for $65 and work began on the new church in the spring of 1916. The funds for the building were raised by pledges. By dedication Sunday, July 30, 1916, a debt of $200 remained, but was paid off by January of 1917. Electric lights were installed with each member contributing $10.

The congregation became a member of the Lutheran Church – Missouri Synod in 1921 when its constitution was presented to the Synodical Convention at Milbank. In 1922 a barn was built on the church property at a cost of $200, with Lane and Forestburg congregations contributing.

German services were held until July of 1923, when it was decided to have an English service twice a month.

In 1968 St. John's Lutheran Church of Lane closed its doors and Zion received the memberships of some of these transfers. Thus Zion and Mount Olive of Woonsocket became a dual parish. The LLL, LWML and Walther League became active mission agencies in the life of the congregation.

Zion Lutheran Church, Stickney, South Dakota

It was 1906 when the Reverend Thusius, pastor of Immanuel Lutheran Church of Dimock started a preaching station in Baker Township, Davison County. Services were held in the homes. In 1914 Zion Lutheran Church of Stickney was organized. The church building was purchased from Immanuel of Dimock when they decided to rebuild their church. The building was moved across the county by a steam engine.

The pastor of Immanuel always served the Zion congregation.

In 1944 the first English service was held at Zion. Sunday School was started in 1951. It's interesting to note that the pastor would take 30 minutes of each of the services for the children in order that he might hear their memory work.

Due to a dwindling membership, the final service of worship and praise of Zion Lutheran Church was held on July 10, 1988 led by Pastor Robert Utecht, then pastor of Immanuel and Zion. Zion had served the community of Stickney for some 74 years.

Redeemer Lutheran Church, Flandreau, South Dakota

Prior to 1916, missionary activity was carried out in the Flandreau and Egan area by the Minnesota District of the Lutheran Church – Missouri Synod. When the time came that the Minnesota District no longer served this area, the South Dakota District of the LC-MS acted to secure a pastor to serve as the first missionary to Moody County. In June of 1917, Martin Keller graduated from Concordia Theological Seminary in St. Louis and received the call to serve in Moody County. As a result of God's blessing upon his work, some two years later Redeemer Lutheran congregation would emerge.

Services were held in the Riverview Township Schoolhouse for these early people. They were also held in the Norwegian church and in the homes of some of the members. In Egan, services were held in the Methodist church as well as the home of the pastor.

On February 8, 1921 Pastor Steinmeyer met with ten men in the home of H. Scharnhorst in order to form a Lutheran Congregation. It was at this meeting that a decision was made to form the congregation in Egan. This was done because it was believed that Egan was the most promising town in the area at that time. It had become a railroad town and two passenger trains were running east and west and two going south to Sioux City and returning each day in the 1890's.

Now a place of worship needed to be found for the new congregation. So late in 1921 a church was purchased from the Methodists in the city of Egan for this purpose. The minutes of the congregation indicate that a committee was authorized to offer from $500 to $600 for the building. The purchase price was $500, of which the congregation received a loan of $200 from the Church Extension Fund. This loan was repaid in 1934 when it became a burden to the young congregation which would face many financial problems.

After Pastor Steinmeyer accepted a call to Pipestone, MN the Reverend John Jungeman of Wolsey was called and accepted that call to serve Redeemer Lutheran Church. His pastorate would extend for nearly 40 years – almost his entire ministry. He also served the Oslo Lutheran Church near Lake Campbell and was instrumental in forming and serving as pastor of Mount Calvary Lutheran Church of Brookings. It's interesting to note in the available history of the congregation that Pastor Jungeman was called to Leola and Long Lake in 1929. But the congregation in a special meeting said that even though these congregations offered a salary of 1,900 dollars annually, if the pastor could get along with his present salary, he should not accept the call. They felt that Egan, being a small congregation, would have a hard time securing a pastor. Pastor Jungeman thus returned the call and remained in Egan. In 1923, the congregation offered its pastor $1,000 which remained the same and was lowered in the coming years. It offered him free rent if the Synod would be willing to assist the congregation financially. (Did anyone say something about dedication to one's ministry????)

The problem that always seemed to plague this young congregation was finances. Early records indicate that Pastor Jungeman had the task of contacting members who had not contributed during the year to make up the deficit. Pastor Jungeman also sold insurance or took over an insurance business and also a filling station which enabled him to meet some of his financial responsibilities.

Redeemer Lutheran became one of the first congregations in the South Dakota District to place the Lutheran Witness in every home.

In 1932 a significant addition was made to the church property, namely, the Egan Opera House was acquired and used as a parish hall. This Opera House was given to the congregation as a gift from a friend of the congregation.

In 1937 Redeemer congregation applied for membership in the Lutheran Church – Missouri Synod.

This was presented to the next convention of the District and accepted. In the mid to late 1950's, the congregation saw that Egan was a community which was not growing. The church was in need of repair and also more room was needed for the congregation. Many of the members of Redeemer were living in Flandreau which caused the congregation to consider moving to Flandreau. It would eliminate the transportation problem for Sunday School, Confirmation instruction, youth activities and Vacation Bible School. When a vote was taken by ballot to move to Flandreau, six votes were in favor of the move and five voted against. A body shop was purchased and was remodeled for a church building for Redeemer. The total cost of the project was $9,000.

The remodeling began on June 24, 1960 with all work, except for the installation of the heat duct, done by volunteer labor.

The first service was held in the new facilities on Easter Sunday, April 2, 1961 conducted by Pastor Jungeman. Dedication services were held on June 4, 1961. After 40 years of faithful service, Pastor Jungeman stepped down as Pastor of Redeemer in June of 1963. Redeemer was later served by the Pastor of Zion of White and First English of Aurora.

Today, Redeemer, Flandreau is served by the pastor from Peace Lutheran Church of Brookings.

Bethesda Lutheran Church, Hot Springs, South Dakota

It was as early as 1896 that a Reverend Lindorfer made a survey of Fall River and Custer counties as well as numerous towns in eastern Wyoming to ascertain the possibility of a church in the area. He performed a baptism at the Huebner Hotel just east of Bethesda's current location.

Since Ardmore seemed the logical place for mission work, the Synod sent the Reverend Elmer Foelber there, where he preached to a group of 12 people on September 10, 1916. Later he conducted services at the Huebner Hotel attended by 20 people and he preached to 16 additional people on September 24th at Edgemont. Junction Schoolhouse northwest of Custer became the setting also for services at this time. In September of 1916 Pastor Foelber began working this entire area in order to ascertain the possibility of starting a congregation. Many discouragements popped up to the pastor when people told him that there was no reason to start a church. However, he was not about to give up at this time. By and by, the number of worshippers increased and the congregation was organized and steps were made to build a church. In March of 1923, 12 voting members decided to build a church and an architect was employed to draw plans for a building 28 x 38 feet to cost about $10,000. The first service was held in this building on December 23, 1923. Dedication of the white stucco building at 207 Charles Avenue (now the corner of Baltimore and 16th) took place June 28, 1924. Many of the people came to the new church from the surrounding areas of Nebraska, Iowa and Minnesota to get relief from their asthma, rheumatism and hay fever. The Pine ozone and mineral-charged warm springs seemed to help in the relief of these ailments. In addition to preaching places at Hot Springs, Ardmore, and Edgemont, Custer was also now given as a possible preaching place. From there he was also invited to the Limestone Region about 10 miles away to hold services. Because the congregation now had its largest membership increase in its 30-year history (435 souls and 276 communicants) the voters decided in December of 1954 to start a building fund. Thus a new A-frame church with seating for 400 was dedicated April 6, 1958.

During the late 1960's and early 1970's the army depot at Igloo was phased out, causing the congregation to experience the removal of a lot of families. A bus was thus purchased for the Walther Leaguers and Release Time children and was also used to bring people from the VA Center and State Soldiers Home to divine services. Prior to Pastor Martin Leedahl's death, discussion began in the congregation on the possibility of starting a Lutheran school.

Thus in 1980, Bethesda Lutheran School was born, opening with grades K-3 and Miss Diane Beaverson as the first called teacher. In 1981, the old church which housed the school was enlarged to provide more space for the school.

Because of the congregation's growth, the church building was now expanded with a 10,000 square foot addition. Dedication took place on March 7, 1993. Most of the labor was provided by Synod's Laborers For Christ program with the assistance of many congregational members. During the 1992-1993 school year the Lutheran School saw its largest enrollment – 49 students. A third full-time teacher was added to the staff at this time. National Lutheran School Accreditation was granted to the school in 1993.

As God continues to bless, Bethesda continues its ministry to the people of the Hot Springs and surrounding communities.

Trinity Lutheran Church, Spencer, South Dakota

According to original records of Trinity Lutheran Church at Spencer, the congregation was in existence back in 1892. The section entitled, "Chronik" gave an account of the early history of the congregation until 1917. However they found no record book for the congregation from 1892 to 1896.

Several Lutheran families that were living in and around Spencer had heard that a Pastor E.G. Stark from Hartford, SD was traveling in the area looking whether he could establish a preaching place. In 1882 he found rich material for establishing such a preaching place at Spencer.

In 1891, Pastor Wilhelm Zabel from Alexandria took over this area with eager and diligent effectiveness. It was during his time here that the congregation was organized and formed on June 6, 1892. The name given to the newly organized congregation was, "The First German Evangelical Lutheran United Congregation in Spencer, McCook County, South Dakota."

Trinity, as it stands today in Spencer, SD

In 1895, Candidate Mr. William Marth was called as pastor at Spencer and to the surrounding area. On October 24, 1897, a regular assembly proposed that with the help of out-of-town brothers they would raise money to build a building in which school and church could be held. Pastor Pfotenhauer, at the time Director of the Minnesota and South Dakota Districts, wrote to several parishes and asked about a collection for the erected church in Spencer.

On February 6, 1898 the congregation moved into its own church and dedicated the same to the service and glory of the Triune God. A house was also needed for the pastor and so a parsonage was then built.

These were years of steady growth for the congregation as the congregation and pastor together had a good relationship in carrying the message of the Gospel to those in the Spencer area. Early records indicate, *"...the congregation loves their pastor and he is a responsible shepherd that takes care of his sheep."*

From its very beginning, Trinity has been concerned about the spiritual welfare of its children. It was in the year 1922 that Pastor Guebert began conducting a Christian Day School in the church building. A building was acquired in 1924 and dedicated for the purpose of educating the children of the congregation. It was in 1930-1931 that adverse financial conditions caused the members to discontinue the school.

Trinity, Spencer, SD following the tornado

Spencer Tornado account as told by Pastor Thomas Christopher:

"May 30, 1998 was the Saturday before Pentecost. I was preparing a sermon on 'the mighty rushing wind,' but never did I imagine I would have such an illustration to go with the words of the text from Acts 2. Wind can be a gentle breeze cooling you on a hot day, or a devastating force tearing apart buildings and killing people. On the evening of May 30, 1998 the devastating force hit Spencer, South Dakota.

"I serve the dual parish of Trinity Lutheran Church in Spencer and St. Martin's Lutheran Church in Alexandria. My family and I live in Alexandria, so we were not in the town of Spencer when the storm hit, although on that evening there were multiple tornadoes in McCook and Hanson

counties and we had spent some time in the basement seeking shelter from a storm near Alexandria.

"*We were out in the front yard of our home watching the clouds after the storm had passed Alexandria, when I learned from a neighbor that Spencer had been 'hit'. I was not immediately too concerned. I had been through tornados before and was expecting there to be some damage, but nothing like what I later would see. I went into the house and called several of the members of Trinity, but only got busy signals, which is what I expected anyway since the tornado would quite likely have knocked out telephone service.*

"*I immediately started out for Spencer. The sun was just setting in the west when I came over the bridge at Spencer Quarry and rounded the curve on Highway 38 expecting to see the town of Spencer standing there to the north as I usually did. Instead, I saw nothing. All the familiar landmarks - the elevator and grain bins, the water tower, even the trees - were gone.*

"*I spent the first few hours on the highway outside of Spencer speaking to and praying with the victims as they were brought out on busses by the emergency workers, all the while making a mental note of the Trinity members who were city residents that I had seen. Thoughts of the church building hardly crossed my mind until later in the evening, after I had begun to get a picture of the devastation by talking to townspeople. The first hint of the fate of the building of Trinity Lutheran Church came from one of our members, Howard Heidelberger, whom I talked to on one of the busses. I will never forget his words: 'My house is gone! My garage is gone! The church is gone! The town is gone! There is nothing left!'*

"*The victims of the storm were all being taken to the armory in Salem until relatives or friends could pick them up. After the busses stopped coming out of Spencer, I went to Salem to continue my visits with the people and to account for several Trinity members whom I had not seen at the highway checkpoint. I finally entered the town of Spencer about 12:30 a.m. There were still a few Trinity members I had to account for, so the first thing I did was to go to their houses to make sure they were not there or help them in some way if they were. I found it hard to make my way around town with only the light of a flashlight to guide me and all the landmarks gone. Fortunately, all the members of Trinity escaped with their lives, although six people were killed in the storm.*

"*When at 3:30 a.m. I finally got to the church building, after having seen the devastation in the rest of the town, I was expecting the worst, and I found it. The building was leveled. I remember thinking as I stood on the top step of the demolished building what a strange and terrible sight this was. The whole scene was eerily back-lit by the emergency lights on Main Street. I remembered the stories my father had told me about the devastated towns he had seen in World War II. I thought that this surely must rival anything that he had seen, and the experience of the tornado survivors must surely have rivaled those of any air-raid survivor. As I stood there, I became aware of the high-pitched beeping of countless smoke alarms buried in the rubble. For some reason that sound struck me as incredibly mournful - the death-knell of a town, sentries sounding the alarm too late. The beeping was heard in Spencer for almost two days after that, until, one by one, the batteries in the alarms went dead.*

"It wasn't until the sun came up that I got a better picture of what hap-pened to the church building. The walls, steeple and bell of the church were thrown to the south and were laying against the parsonage which stood not 30 feet from the church building. All of the items inside the building, however, were thrown to the north and the east - the pews all broken and laying in a pile on the north of the building and the chancel furnishings all laying to the east. The beautiful stained-glass windows for which Trinity was known now consisted of small pieces of broken glass scattered all about the site.

"I'm sure I could fill tens of pages with a description of the events that followed and the things the members of Trinity saw and did following the storm. Through it all, however, it is easy to see God's grace and pro-tective mercy upon His people. Stories of miraculous survival abounded - one woman surviving a several block trip through town courtesy of the tornado wind, another woman, unable to get to her basement, sitting in her chair in the living room praying as her house came apart around her (she survived with barely a scratch).

"The members of Trinity Lutheran Church, however, were determined that the ministry of Word and Sacrament would go on in Spencer, South Da-kota. On the Wednesday following the storm they held a worship service of praise and thanksgiving in the city park. This was perhaps the largest worship service Trinity had ever held, with hundreds of people, rescue workers and citizens of the community, joining the members of Trinity in singing the praises of God who gave us our town and is blessed even when He takes it away.

"The Sunday following the storm was a bittersweet day in the history of the congregation. We were again joined by hundreds of people as we held the final worship service on the floor of the old church building. After the elders and officers of the congregation came forward and, one by one, took out the sacred items that we could salvage - the communion vessels, the altar crucifix, etc. - with many tears we decommissioned the building and gave her into the hands of our loving God. Two days later she was bulldozed, pushed into a hole and buried.

"By the next Sunday we had procured a large yellow tent and the ministry of Word and Sacrament continued in the Spencer park. Every Sunday the men would come early and put up the tent and take it down again after the service. We worshiped in that tent in the park for the whole summer of 1998. God provided for us even there. On many Sunday mornings I would wake up to pouring rain thinking it was going to be a miserable day in the park, but as the time for putting up the tent approached the rain would stop and it wouldn't start again until the tent was down and put away!

"By two weeks after the storm, the members of Trinity had determined they were going to rebuild the church in Spencer. After the tent, our first sanctuary was Howard and Bev Heidelberger's new garage. Ground was

broken for the new church building and on June 6, 1999 - one year almost to the day after decommissioning the old building, the new building of Trinity Lutheran Church in Spencer was dedicated to the glory of God. Again we had a large number of guests - over 600 people joined us on that day to dedicate our new building.

"Today, although the numbers are not so large, the congregation of Trinity continues to worship in Spencer. The city of Spencer recently celebrated its 125th anniversary. By God's grace may Trinity congregation continue the ministry of God's Word in the community of Spencer for the next 125 years."

Trinity Lutheran Church, Reliance, South Dakota

It was in the fall of 1908 that congregations of Red Lake, West Point and Reliance called the Reverend Martin Engel to minister to the Lutherans in these areas. Pastor Engel lived in Chamberlain and served both sides of the Missouri River. In 1917 the congregations of Red Lake, Westpoint and Chamberlain merged into one congregation and Reliance was left with a decision to make.

On May 27, 1917 families met in what was known as the Lebselter Schoolhouse southeast of Reliance to organize a Lutheran Church. At this meeting, a number of families decided that it was time that they started a church. Thus was the beginning of the Trinity Lutheran Church of Reliance.

In October of 1917 the building was completed and listed its expenses; "lumber $821.70; drugstore $9.85; carpet $30.30; hardware $35; making a total cost of $896.85 of which $199.45 was unpaid, all labor had been donated." Even the altar cloths were sewn by the ladies of the congregation.

The church was formally dedicated to the glory of God on October 14, 1917 under the guidance of Reverend Fredricksen.

In 1918, the by-laws were discussed and the church constitution was adopted. Money was raised to pay off the debts and to purchase a bell. (This bell is still in use today, calling people to worship each Sunday.) In 1920, communion vessels were purchased and a formal decision was made to unite with the Lutheran Church – Missouri Synod.

Trinity was served for a short time by the pastor from Presho and formed a dual parish in 1936.

A new church was built on land that was donated by A.C. Miller in Reliance for the future church site. The church was built and dedicated to the glory of God on July 18, 1954. This new house of worship cost about $5,300.

Trinity of Reliance was linked with Presho a number of different times, until in 1973 it again formed a dual parish which is still in existence today.

As one reads the history of Trinity, Reliance it has had its full share of trials and tests. And yet the people acknowledge that it was help from Almighty

God which sustained them throughout these trials and tribulations and gave them the wisdom and fortitude to grow and thrive in the midst of all these problems.

Zion Lutheran Church, Chamberlain, South Dakota

The early history of Zion Lutheran Church can be written in terms of hardships experienced by a few of the missionaries, the first of which to visit the city of Chamberlain was the Reverend A.H. Kuntz. He was installed in the church in White Lake and later served the Ola and Red Lake areas and finally Westpoint as preaching stations. A lot of work was done in the Red Lake, Westpoint and Pukwana areas before Candidate Frank Albrecht from the St. Louis Seminary was called to serve. He remained until 1903 and was succeeded by R. G. Runge.

In 1917 the decision was made to merge the congregations at Red Lake, Westpoint and Chamberlain into one. The church building at the Red Lake site (originally from Pukwana) was moved into Chamberlain and Zion Lutheran congregation was formed on December 30, 1917. The congregation joined the Lutheran Church – Missouri Synod on August 22, 1920.

Zion Lutheran Church at Chamberlain in the middle of adding a Fellowship hall. Work provided by laborers for Christ and funded by the SD District Church Extension Fund.

A milestone was reached when on June 25, 1950 the present house of worship was dedicated as the place of worship of their God by the people of the Chamberlain area. Property north of the church was partially purchased and partially donated in 1966 on which today is located a beautiful kitchen, fellowship hall and Sunday School rooms. The people of Zion, Chamberlain recognize that God receives all glory and honor for what has all happened in their lives because of His ministry to them these many years.

Trinity Lutheran Church for the Deaf, Sioux Falls, South Dakota

The Reverend John L. Salvenor, missionary to the deaf in the Minneapolis, MN area visited the state school for the deaf in Sioux Falls in the years 1902, 1903 and 1904. Even though the last service which he held showed 40 in attendance, the pressing load of work in the twin cities area prohibited further visits to the Sioux Falls area.

In 1918, Pastor Salvenor met with a deaf woman of Sioux Falls in a Duluth, Minnesota Deaf service. Through this woman's pleading for services like this in Sioux Falls it was learned that all the Sioux Falls deaf desired services in the future. Thus the first service was held October 10, 1918. Fifty people were in attendance, including 30 people from the South Dakota School for the Deaf. Services were held every month and some of the pupils always attended. On June 11-17, 1919 the South Dakota District met in convention in Sioux Falls and a joint service was conducted attended by the delegates and a number of deaf.

Pastor Matthew Nix's ordination/installation as pastor at Trinity for the Deaf - July 18, 1993 (pastor Tim Rynearson, Pastor Steve Gallo, Pastor Nix, Dr. Rodney Rynearson, and President Raymond Hartwig.

In October of 1919 the first class of adult deaf was confirmed at Trinity.

Other stations were added in the course of time. On September 13, 1921 the first service was held in Watertown, SD with seven deaf in attendance. The first service in Mitchell, SD was held on April of 1924 and in the January service of 1926 one deaf man had come 140 miles for service and instruction. In March of 1925, it was reported that 11 deaf were taking instructions preparatory for confirmation.

By 1927 there were 26 communicants in Sioux Falls, nine in Mitchell and four in the Ortonville, MN area.

In January of 1928, the Reverend Ernest Mappes of Omaha began to serve Sioux Falls and Mitchell, while Pastor Salvenor continued to serve the other stations. In 1928 services also began in the Aberdeen area with ten deaf in attendance.

In 1938, the Reverend Arnold T. Jonas was installed on January 9th in Sioux Falls. Thirty-five deaf attended the service. Average attendance of 35 was now stable following Pastor Jonas' installation.

On January 10, 1943 the second resident pastor, the Reverend Arnold J. Lutz was installed in this field. He preached to the deaf in South Dakota stations as well as Montevideo, MN. He also served the deaf in Duluth, MN and Superior, WI.

In 1944 Candidate Curtis Schleicher, a graduate of the Springfield Seminary was ordained and installed in Sioux Falls on July 30, 1944. In January 1945, ten stations comprised the Sioux Falls field: Sioux Falls, Big Stone City, Watertown, Aberdeen, Mitchell and Yankton, South Dakota as well as Montevideo and Albert Lee in Minnesota and Mason City and Waterloo in Iowa. Services were held in Sioux Falls three times a month and once a month in the other cities.

It was on October 27, 1947 that ground was purchased for a chapel in Sioux Falls across from the Deaf School. This project was supported to a large degree by the Lutheran Women's Missionary League of the South Dakota District LCMS. The title to the property was in the name of the South Dakota District of The Lutheran Church – Missouri Synod. The chapel was completed and dedicated for use for services for the deaf on December 18, 1949. Thus the members of Trinity Lutheran Church for the Deaf, though small in number, have maintained their own building.

On October 30, 1947 Trinity Lutheran Church for the Deaf was organized with seven voters and 26 communicants, including those at the school.

In 1952 the Reverend Robert F. Cordus was called from St. Paul, MN and installed in Sioux Falls.

In 1963 the Reverend George Ring, who had served the Oregon field, was called to serve at Trinity in Sioux Falls.

As the building became older and in need of much repair, the South Dakota District Board of Directors proposed that Trinity Lutheran Church for the Deaf join with Christ Lutheran Church, which also was looking for a new facility to become a new mission congregation on the east side of Sioux Falls. Thus the building was built for Christ Lutheran with a Chapel added for Trinity Lutheran Church for the Deaf. This was in 1995-1996. Since that time Pastor Matthew Nix, District Missionary for the Deaf, has served as pastor to Trinity Lutheran.

Our Redeemer Lutheran Church, Philip, South Dakota

In the early 1900's, a number of Lutheran families settled on homesteads south of Philip. Thus was the beginning of the "German Lutheran Church of

Philip." These people were first served by Circuit Riders. In 1906, Reverend M.G. Pollack served Philip and Cottonwood.

The first resident pastor was C.F. Kellermann, a graduate of Concordia Seminary in St. Louis, MO.

Since there were no organized congregations and a parsonage was needed, a corporation was formed on September 7, 1919. The official title of the church was, "The Evangelical Lutheran Church of Our Redeemer of the Evangelical Lutheran Synod of Missouri, Ohio and Other States." The basic reason for this corporation was for the purpose of purchasing a parsonage for the resident pastor. This was accomplished on May 20, 1920 for the sum of $2,500.

Pastor Kellermann often held confirmation classes in the shade beside a haystack. In 1923 he accepted a call to Mansfield, SD and the congregation was then served by Pastor Andrew Szegedin.

Pre-School at Our Redeemer Lutheran Church, Philip, SD

In 1939 a church building was purchased from the Methodists from Ottumwa. Two lots were purchased on Oak Street and West Avenue. A basement was completed and the cornerstone was laid. Placed in the cornerstone was a Bible, Hymn Book, a Catechism, the names of the communicant members, the name of the President of the United States, the Governor's name, the mayor's name, a copy of the Constitution of the Church, and a copy of the state and county newspapers. The church was then moved on May 3, 1940. During this time an accident happened which put Henry Kurth, (a member) in the hospital. As he was pulling the church behind his tractor down a steep hill, some of the retaining wires gave way and the church rolled up onto the tractor, pinning Henry against the steering wheel. God soon returned him to good health.

On August 2, 1940 the church was dedicated to God's glory and honor and for the worship of His holy name.

In April of 1993 discussions began about the possibility of beginning a pre-school. It was decided to begin the preschool in January 1994. The first year showed sixteen students and two teachers – Mrs. Amy Kroetsch and Miss Angela Walker.

St. John Lutheran Church, Norris, South Dakota

The early history of the St. John congregation is quite interesting. The original membership was made up of mainly ethnic German people, most of whom were immigrants or sons and daughters of immigrants who came from Germany. Most came to the United States after almost a generation in Russia, Bulgaria, Switzerland or Poland.

In the mid 1800's an increasingly militant Prussia resulted in that country being dominated by a military elite with all the young men being drafted into the Army.

The history of German settlements in Russia really begins with the reign of Czarina Catherina II, also called Catherine the Great (1762-1796). Following the example of Czarina Catherina, his grandmother, Czar Alexander I offered incentives to colonists who would come into and develop the land in Bessarabia, the Ukraine and the Crimea, in southern Russia. This area bordered Turkey and the Turks were warlike and hostile to their neighbors. The German and Swiss people came in great numbers and, as they were ambitious and hard-working, they prospered for more than fifty years. Unfortunately under Czar Alexander II all the incentives to the settlers were cancelled and all young men were subject to military service. Thus the Germans began looking for a new land to settle and most came to the United States and Canada. Many of the immigrants came to eastern South Dakota and northeastern Nebraska to friends and relatives and from there made the move to Mellette and Todd Counties. As they came west they brought with them their language, customs, and religion. Wherever a few came together, they formed congregations and established churches.

Previous to 1918, the general triangle bounded by Cedar Butte, Parmelee and Norris had two Lutheran congregations: Immanuel and St. John. Immanuel services were held in a building of sod blocks. A wooden box covered with black cloth served as an altar. Planks served as pews and a small coal heater was used for warmth. This was the church serving the southern part of the triangle.

St. John, comprised mostly of the people living north of the county line, held services in the Bernard Galster home – a log house. The kitchen stove served as altar and people sat wherever they could, including the bedroom. In 1917, the members decided to build a church and in 1918 a church was completed at the present site on land donated by Gottlieb Schmidt. St. John received the land deed on February 15, 1919 as well as the charter on November 3, 1919. This is presently St. John Lutheran Church of Norris, South Dakota.

St. John congregation still serves the people in this windswept area of South Dakota on the open plains. Its steeple points heavenward, always reminding its worshippers of the God whom they serve as well as the God who watches over them each step of the way.

Zion Lutheran Church, Presho, South Dakota

The foundation of Zion Lutheran Church of Presho began in 1909 when the Mission Board sent Reverend Gustav Steffen to Draper, SD searching for Lutherans. He found a number of families who were interested in having church services, even if it were just occasionally. Arrangements were made with the school board to hold services at the Schoelte School located about 15 miles southwest of Presho.

On December 25, 1910 a children's Christmas program was held. What a wonderful event for the children who had never seen a Christmas tree with lighted candles; perhaps it had other decorations too. Gifts and treats were received. The building was packed with people.

This group of Lutherans then organized and on June 19, 1911 received the Articles of Incorporation from the State of South Dakota and became known as Evangelical Lutheran Bethlehem Congregation.

In the early 1900's services were held in the old Norwegian church across the tracks where the sale barn stands. The following years showed children being confirmed and the congregation showing growth. Services were often held in homes of members and in later years were conducted in schoolhouses once a month. Quite often these services were held in the afternoon. Many of the services were held in the Cedar Valley School, Kincannon School and Brule School. About 1935, the Lutheran members started coming into Presho to attend services and participate in the activities of the church.

Church services were also held in Vivian from 1915 to probably the early 1930's.

On October 10, 1920 the congregation was formally organized. The first constitution was adopted on October 24, 1920 thereby creating Zion Evangelical Lutheran Church of Presho, SD. Today Presho and Reliance are served by one pastor as they form a parish.

Chapter 10
1920-1930

Messiah Lutheran Church, Murdo, South Dakota

In the early 1900's the area around Murdo began to grow. However, the drought years were very difficult years for these struggling Lutherans. In 1906 Pastor Gade was instrumental in gathering hearers and conducting services in both the German and English language to around 30-40 hearers, often in homes or rented halls.

About 1920, under Reverend Walter G. Goings' supervision, the Messiah congregation was officially organized. Pastor O.E. Reimnitz was the first pastor to occupy the newly built parsonage.

On August 3, 1952 many prayers were answered and a new church was dedicated. Pastor O.M. Schultz was installed on that same day and the Murdo-Draper parish was formed.

First English Lutheran Church, Aurora, South Dakota

In the year 1922, Lutheran services in English were rare in Brookings County. Norwegian or Danish were used in several places. At Elkton, White and Argo, German was the principal language.

A request was made to the Mission Board of the South Dakota District of the Wisconsin Synod for a pastor. The Reverend Edward R. Blakewell, a seminary candidate, was commissioned as Missionary by the Wisconsin Synod to the area of Brookings. A formal meeting was held on March 22, 1923 for the purpose of organizing a church. The name chosen for the new congregation was First English Lutheran.

Worship services were held and the decision was made to construct a church in the amount of $3,900. The cornerstone for the new church was laid on Pentecost Day, May 20, 1923. This new church was then dedicated on September 23. The new congregation applied for membership in the Evangelical Lutheran Joint Synod of Wisconsin and other States on April 13, 1924. This application was accepted by the District at its convention on June 18, 1924.

Now came the problem of the debt. By a vote of 16-0 it was decided that each member raise and contribute one hog toward the liquidation of the debt for the church. Thus a "Pig Committee" came into existence. The following quote from their history is interesting:

> "...when building the church we were obliged to assume a considerable debt. To lessen the debt we came up with the idea of Pig Day. Once a year each farmer was asked to donate a pig to pay the debt. We did this a number of years. Then we began donating money instead of pigs and the name changed to Pay Day. Some day in the winter would be selected and we would have a social gathering, a supper and a program. For many years these gatherings were eagerly looked forward to. In 1944 our debt was finally liquidated."

At a special meeting on April 25, 1949 the congregation voted to join the Missouri Synod and asked Pastor Victor Lemke of White to serve them as vacancy pastor. The date is not given for their acceptance by the LCMS, but it was probably at its convention in 1949. First English joined as a dual parish with Zion Lutheran Church of White. In 1951 the parish agreement was broken and First English joined with Mount Calvary of Brookings as a dual parish. On June 28, 1970 First English joined once again with White as a dual parish which is still in existence today.

God's blessings have been abundant on First English Lutheran Church. May His blessings continue in the future!

St. Paul's Lutheran Church, Leola, South Dakota

It was the year 1922 – the great war to end all wars had just ended. The mood in America was one of hope and optimism.

This optimism also carried itself into the Dakota farm country. Things seemed to be looking up. Hard times were now going to be a thing of the past. Blizzards, drought, dust bowl days – all seemed to be things that would be left behind. The future was full of promise. Doctors were becoming more numerous and education was available for all children. Automobiles were becoming more numerous, as were electric lights, indoor plumbing and graveled streets.

This optimism also filled the people around Leola, South Dakota. They were without a church home but did not become discouraged and pessimistic. Through their hard work and the leadership of a dedicated pastor they put themselves to the task of building a new church home.

Even though St. Paul's Lutheran Church was organized in 1922, work had begun already the year before when eleven families from the Leola area held their first worship service on July 17, 1921 with Pastor P.L. Kluender leading. Pastor Kluender was from Christ Lutheran Church in Albion Township of North Dakota, nine miles northwest of Ellendale. These services were held in the movie theatre. As this group grew, they officially began to function as a congregation on October 23, 1921, numbering approximately 70 people.

Since Pastor Kluender was already serving five other congregations besides the one in Leola, it was necessary that the people of Leola find another means of ministry in their midst. They found that Immanuel congregation in Long Lake, South Dakota (which Pastor Kluender was serving as a vacancy), was willing to join with them in forming a dual parish and calling a pastor. So on January 25, 1922 the Reverend A. Merkens of Scobey, Montana, a missionary at large for the North Dakota-Montana District, was called as pastor. He was installed as pastor of the two congregations on Rogate Sunday, May 21, 1922.

On June 4, 1922, Pentecost Sunday, a constitution was adopted and St. Paul's Lutheran Church joined with the other congregations of the Lutheran Church – Missouri Synod at a regular convention at Tripp, South Dakota.

On June 5, 1922 the congregation decided to build a church in order to get out of the local movie theatre. Four lots were purchased on the main street of town (the present site of the church) for $364. On August 6, 1922 the cornerstone was laid. The members did much of the work in building the church, hauling gravel and rock and working at erecting the building itself. The cost of the building was approximately $10,000, a rather large sum for such a small congregation. They raised $6,000 of the needed money very soon after building.

On November 19, 1922 the completed building was dedicated. Even though the congregation had its own building, the real work of the church had just begun. The first period of time tended to be very difficult as the language question caused difficulty and the matter of lodge membership needed to be settled. But according to God's good and gracious will and blessings, the membership of the congregation grew rapidly during Pastor Merkens' seven years in Leola. Various pastors served prior to 1964 when Good Shepherd Lutheran Church of Ipswich was aligned with the Leola congregation and formed a parish. Pastor Raymond Hartwig, (former South Dakota District President, now Secretary of the Lutheran Church – Missouri Synod) was installed on August 27, 1971 and served this parish until August of 1974. The Reverend Ray Pomplun was installed on September 28, 1986. Pastor Pomplun retired in the summer of 2005.

First Lutheran Church, Milesville, South Dakota

Mission work began in the Milesville area in 1907 when missionaries served a wide area in western South Dakota. Services were held in the homes of families who attended. These areas involved Milesville, Elbon, Quinn, Pedro, Philip and Creighton.

On February 11, 1923, Pastor C.F. Kellerman suggested that a Lutheran congregation be organized at Milesville. A decision was made the next day to organize that congregation and a constitution was presented on March 4, 1923 which was adopted. The name of the congregation was First Evangelical Lutheran Church of Milesville. The members voted to apply for membership in the Lutheran Church – Missouri Synod on November 10, 1925. Now came the need for a building for worship. A meeting was held on May 16, 1926. A one acre plot of land was given to the church. The congregation decided to build on October 22, 1929. A building 22 feet by 34 feet and a tower was built in 1930 and dedicated to God's glory and for His worship and praise.

On May 16, 1958 it was decided to build an extra twenty feet on the south side of the church. It was also in 1958 that the church basement was finished.

A new addition on the northeast corner of the church was built in 1979 to serve as an emergency fire escape.

First Lutheran Church, Milesville, SD

Because of dwindling population in the area, as well as declining church membership, First Evangelical Lutheran Church of Milesville was closed on September 12, 2003.

St. John's Lutheran Church, Tyndall, South Dakota

The exact date of organization of St. John's of Tyndall cannot be determined from records available. More recent reports seem to indicate that the congregation was organized in 1924. Several attempts were made from 1901 to 1925 to establish a Lutheran church in Tyndall with little success.

In 1925 the Reverend J.C. Hildebrandt of Menno came to Tyndall to establish a congregation. He located a number of people who were members of Lutheran churches in the area. Under his leadership the congregation soon numbered 40 people. His first sermon was preached in September of 1925 in the Presbyterian church, rented for $1.50 per service.

With the advice of the Mission Board, St. John's participated with Zion Lutheran Church in Avon in calling the Reverend O.W. Matthies to serve them as pastor in 1927.

The first resident pastor of St. John's was the Reverend E.F. Bergmann who was installed in August of 1931 and served the congregation for two years. In March of 1934 a new constitution was adopted and services were still being held in the Presbyterian church. With the aid of a $1,250 loan from the District, in December of 1940 the congregation purchased the German Congregational church property in Tyndall. In 1942 under the leadership of Pastor R.A. Wegener, the church property was renovated, improved and dedicated to the service of the Triune God on October 4, 1942.

The congregation then purchased a church building from the Eigenfeld Lutheran Church in March 1951 for $5,400. This church was located southwest of Parkston and had originally been moved from Armour, South Dakota. The old church was sold and moved. Groundbreaking for the new church was held on May 27, 1951.

The cornerstone for the new church building was laid on October 21, 1951 and dedicated on October 18, 1953.

On Sunday, June 19, 1994 St. John's Lutheran dedicated a new house of worship to be used in the proclamation of the Gospel and various church functions. This new facility well meets the needs of the congregation as it continues to proclaim the Gospel of Jesus Christ to the people of Tyndall and surrounding community.

Emmanuel Lutheran Church, Gettysburg, South Dakota

Lutheran church services have been conducted in Gettysburg since 1909. Formal organization of Emmanuel Lutheran Church took place on October 15, 1925 under the leadership of Reverend F.A. Hinners. On January 15, 1928 Reverend H.M. Bauer was installed as pastor. He resided in Agar. On July 1, 1928 Pembroke was added to the parish.

In 1931, the basement church was built for use by the congregation. It was located south of the present Catholic classroom building. Men donated their time to building while the women provided the funds through their Ladies Aid organization. Eventually a church was built on the basement and dedication took place on November 11, 1931. Various pastors served over the years, one of which was Pastor O.D. Brack who was installed on March 21, 1948. On August 31, 1948 excavation was started and the formal cornerstone-laying service was held the first Sunday of advent that same year. A basement was dug and seating capacity of 280 was available in the new church. Dedication services were held on June 26, 1949. In the fall of 1952, construction was started on the parsonage with dedication on October 18, 1953.

In 1955 Pembroke disbanded and the members joined Emmanuel at Gettysburg.

On October 5, 1958 Reverend Robert E. Utecht was installed and served for 16 years. The Sunday School building was added on March 10, 1963.

God's blessings still attend this congregation serving the people in the northern part of our South Dakota District.

Mount Calvary Lutheran Church, Huron, South Dakota

Mission work began in Huron in September of 1926. The first worship services were held in the American Legion Hall on November 7, 1926. Twelve people were in attendance. As the attendance grew, the congregation was formally organized on February 12, 1927. Property was purchased at Dakota Avenue and 11th Street Southwest for a new church building. On November 13, 1927 the new church building was dedicated.

Under God's rich blessings, the congregation continued to grow. A building committee was formed in 1947 to look at the possibility of building a large and permanent structure for the worship of almighty God in the city of Huron. The current site at 7th and Dakota Avenue South was purchased in 1950. Ground was broken on Palm Sunday, April 13, 1955 and a new church building was dedicated to God's glory on August 12, 1956. The need for educational facilities was recognized. Having used a home, it was now time for something more permanent and feasible to be found. So in the spring of 1981 funds were gathered for the purpose of building a new educational building together with fellowship space and office facilities. On Easter Sunday, April 3, 1988 ground was broken for this new fellowship hall and church offices. The new addition was dedicated on Reformation Sunday, October 30, 1988.

During the summer of 1989 the church basement was remodeled to provide an education area with permanent Sunday School classrooms. The new educational facilities were dedicated on Rally Day, September 10, 1989.

Over the years, God has abundantly blessed Mount Calvary Lutheran Church with the faithful proclamation of His word and the administration of the sacraments. The congregation numbers some 1,000 baptized souls. Various pastors have served Mount Calvary, among whom are former President Reverend Philip H. Mueller. It is presently being served by the Reverend Dale Sattgast, First Vice President of our District.

St. John's Lutheran Church, Emery, South Dakota

St. John's Lutheran Church was organized on January 17, 1926 with four charter families. Pastor Edward Dewald was called as the first minister.

At a joint meeting of St John's congregation of Emery and St. Martin's of Alexandria on January 24, 1943, St. John's unanimously declared a willingness to join its sister congregation in calling a Pastor who would jointly serve the two congregations. During the years 1944 and 1945 the church building was enlarged and many improvements were made to the building itself. The enlarged house of worship was dedicated on September 16, 1945.

In the fall of 1981 the Alexandria/Emery parish was dissolved. New parishes were formed with Alexandria and Spencer becoming a dual parish and Emery and Clayton becoming a dual parish.

The congregation is served today by Pastor John T.P. Werner who accepted the call to Emery and Clayton and was installed on August 28, 1994. Pastor Werner is a native South Dakotan from the Wall area.

Mount Olive Lutheran Church, Woonsocket, South Dakota

Prior to Mount Olive Lutheran Church being built in Woonsocket, the Lutheran families from that vicinity attended services at Lane, South Dakota. Services were then held in Woonsocket in May, 1927.

Mount Olive Lutheran Church was officially organized on April 7, 1929 when the constitution and by-laws were read and adopted at a regular meeting.

Dedication of the Mount Olive Lutheran Church building at that time was held on June 21, 1931.

In 1938 the suggestion was made by the District that Wessington Springs, Lane and Woonsocket call a pastor for all three churches. On August 21, 1938 a call was extended to Reverend Steve Persa. He accepted that call and began serving the three congregations.

In May of 1947 a meeting was called by the congregations at Lane, Wessington Springs, rural Forestburg and Woonsocket to discuss the formation of two parishes made up of Wessington Springs/Lane and Forestburg/Woonsocket.

In 1969 Mount Olive and Bethlehem separated. Mount Olive, Woonsocket combined with Zion, Wessington Springs to call a pastor.

A Ladies Aid Society was organized in May of 1933 and in 1943 joined the Lutheran Women's Missionary League. This society is responsible for many gifts to the congregation, i.e., altar paraments, dossal curtain, American and Christian flags and a large Altar Bible, just to name a few.

With the closing of St. John's Lutheran Church at Lane in 1969 and Bethlehem rural Forestburg in 1971, Mount Olive gained a number of new members. The original building was therefore sold to the Assembly of God congregation in 1971 and the present building was given to Mount Olive by Bethlehem, Forestburg. Originally this church was purchased near Tulare in 1943, torn down and rebuilt at its location 15 miles northeast of Woonsocket. It was dedicated on June 2, 1946. Then on February 25, 1971 the church was moved to its present site on lots which were given to the congregation by Mrs. Elsie Cook.

Among the many faithful servants who served Mount Olive was the Reverend Paul G. Wendling, a candidate from the St. Louis Seminary who later became District President.

Mount Calvary Lutheran Church, Brookings, South Dakota

Missouri Synod Lutherans coming from Minnesota could find no congregation affiliated in the Brookings area with the Lutheran Church – Missouri Synod, thus they appealed to their pastor, the Reverend J.G. Steinmeyer who discussed the situation with the Mission Boards of the Minnesota and South Dakota Districts. The latter requested the Reverend John Jungeman of Egan to begin mission work in Brookings. The first service was conducted May 15, 1927 in the Sellars-Bartling Funeral home on Williams Street. Eighteen people were in attendance, the offering amounted to $3.50 and the rent for the facility was $7.50.

A Candidate for the ministry from Concordia Seminary in St. Louis was called in the person of Arthur H. Laesch and installed as the first resident pastor on September 9, 1928. He was to also take care of the spiritual needs of the Lutheran students attending South Dakota State College. The congregation was then organized on October 21, 1928 with four members signing the constitution.

In June of 1930 the congregation moved to a new place of worship, namely the basement of the Public Library. This was used free of charge until the fall of 1931 when the Library Board requested $5.99 rent per service.

The inadequacy of temporary places for worship as well as increasing membership caused the church to consider its own home for worship. The Mission Board of the South Dakota District granted the congregation a loan and two lots were bought on the corner of 8th Street and 5th Avenue. On October 22, 1934, ground was broken for a building which was to be a combination church and parsonage. A large part of the work was donated by the members under the supervision of Mr. Emil Olson. December 9, 1934 the cornerstone was laid and on the 31st of March 1935 the building was dedicated to God's glory. Due to the cooperation of the members, total cost for house and church was a very modest $5,000.

At the Voters' Meeting on April 19, 1936 the congregation voted to become a member of the Lutheran Church – Missouri Synod and signed the constitution of Synod later that year. Through the efforts of various pastors over the years, ministry was also done on the South Dakota State campus. The District LWML extended a grant of $3,000 to the congregation to establish a Student Center in a corner of the church basement. Thus the college students were able to come over to the church not only for fun and games, but also for Bible study and for studying for their various classes. They became affiliated with the Gamma Delta Student organization of our church and were known as the Beta Psi Chapter.

Mount Calvary Lutheran Church today still serves the people of the Brookings area as well as Lutheran students at South Dakota State University.

Redeemer Lutheran Church, Doland

The first mission efforts in the vicinity of Doland were short-lived and indicative of the difficulty that the congregation faced during these early years. In the 1880's services were held somewhat irregularly in a school house ten miles southwest of Doland. Pastor Cloeter of Wolsey and Pastor Fritz conducted services but the mission was given up because of difficulties over the Lodge question. Almost 50 years passed before anything happened again.

In 1928 Doland and the vicinity in eastern Spink county was canvassed by Reverend G.H. Steffen who served as missionary at large in South Dakota at that time. In the summer of 1930 the Mission Board called Candidate Paul

Brill, a graduate of Concordia Seminary, St. Louis, MO who was ordained and installed on November 9, 1930. During his pastorate the church building in Doland was purchased with the help of a District Church Extension Fund loan. The congregation was organized and joined Synod at this time.

In 1934 the Redfield mission was combined with Doland and was served by Pastor Beisel.

Redeemer congregation still continues to serve faithfully the people of the Doland area and is a dual parish with the Redfield congregation.

Faith Lutheran Church, Sioux Falls, South Dakota

In the late 1920's, the South Dakota District of the Lutheran Church – Missouri Synod adopted a resolution to carry out a more extensive mission program within the state giving special attention to the larger cities. Thus it was in 1928 that the District called the Reverend G. H. Steffen to serve as Missionary-at-Large in the State of South Dakota and directed him to make a survey and to canvass the east side of Sioux Falls. The result of these decisions and activity was the establishment of Faith Lutheran Mission.

The new congregation was to be "a daughter of Zion." This was not only in a spiritual sense but also literally. The members of Zion gave their support to the establishment of a new mission on the east side by giving a number of members to serve as a core group for the new mission congregation.

The District acquired property at the corner of Cliff Avenue and 4th Street and built a chapel with two wings to serve as classrooms for a Christian Day School. The cornerstone was laid on October 25, 1929 and the new house of worship and school facilities were dedicated on a cold and blustery day in November of 1929.

At a regular Voters' Meeting on May 17, 1931 members of the District Mission Board were asked to be present for the purpose of calling a pastor. The result of the balloting was that Pastor G.H. Steffen was elected without a dissenting vote and installed as first pastor of the congregation and as teacher of the parish school.

By 1962 it became apparent that the congregation's physical facilities did not provide sufficient space to take care of all the Sunday School classes demanded by the number of people in attendance. In order to conduct the VBS sessions in the summer of 1962 it was necessary to erect a spacious tent to house a number of classes. So in January of 1963 a resolution was passed to form a building committee which would interview architects. By January 1967 Parezo and Massa were engaged to make drawings of a Sunday School wing. During this time, Pastor Gehrke received and accepted a call away from Faith and Pastor O.D. Brack of St. Paul's, Aberdeen accepted the call to become pastor of Faith Lutheran Church.

In the fall of 1967 the building committee came to the conclusion that it was advisable to construct a completely new plant.

On September 22, after the 11 a.m. service the congregation assembled on the church grounds formerly used as the parking lot and, at a point that is now the center of the sanctuary, the ground-breaking ceremony was conducted. On May 26, 1969 the cornerstone was laid in the new building and on July 27, 1969 the dedication of the new church facilities was held.

Faith Lutheran Church is a member congregation of the Sioux Falls Lutheran School Association and in 2004 celebrated its 75th anniversary. God has truly blessed Faith Lutheran as it continues to grow and increase not only numerically but also spiritually in the Word!

First Evangelical Lutheran Church, Wall, South Dakota

Early records of the history of First Evangelical Lutheran Church are scant and so the founding of First Lutheran Church is difficult to pinpoint. We know that much missionary work was done by pioneer pastors and early residents, especially those at St. Paul Lutheran Church located 14 miles north of Quinn. Among the first was Pastor G. Schaeffer who established a mission post in the town of Quinn preaching in the Methodist church. Quinn at that time was the largest town in the area. Unfortunately, his work was disrupted by World War I. Later Pastor A.W. Kraft accepted a call to St. Paul of Quinn in May of 1930. Pastor Kraft established a mission station in the town of Wall with services being held in the Methodist church. First Lutheran Church had its beginnings during these years and is greatly indebted to the Lutheran church at Quinn (which is no longer in existence) and Creighton for the missionary pastor's support.

In the Spring of 1946 a former Presbyterian church was purchased in Philip by the congregation and moved and set on a basement foundation on lots next to the parsonage. The first service in this church was December 25, 1946 with dedication held in 1950.

At the annual meeting, January 2, 1957 a committee was set up to investigate the possibilities of a new church. The adjacent 1 1/2 lots had been purchased in 1956. By February of 1958 a decision was made by the members to build a new church located on the corner of the three present lots owned by the congregation. The total cost for the new church was $65,000. The new brick building was dedicated on May 3, 1959.

First Evangelical Lutheran Church of Wall was incorporated in January, 1972, at which time it adopted restated articles of incorporation and revised the by-laws. New classrooms were added and were first used in the fall of

1979.

On September 11, 1983 the education wing and bell tower were dedicated to the Lord with a consecration service led by Reverend John T.P. Werner.

Chapter 11
1930-1950

Messiah Lutheran Church, Redfield, South Dakota

Messiah Lutheran Church of Redfield was established in 1931. Services were first held in the city hall, later in the Syndicate Building and for 15 years in a small frame church they purchased. They are now held in a modern brick structure.

The first pastor to serve Messiah was the Reverend C.A. Mennicke who served from October 11, 1931 to June 24, 1934. Pastor Ruben C. Beisel served from July 1, 1934 to November 14, 1937.

In 1938 the Reverend Hugo Larson was installed and served until 1945. Pastor Larson also served Redeemer at Doland. At that time the parish included Zion at Rockham, Messiah at Redfield and Redeemer at Doland.

On May 3, 1946 a Christian Scientist Church was purchased and under the guidance of Reverend H.H. Kuehn, Messiah Lutheran Church was organized and incorporated earlier that same year.

In the summer of 1961 Messiah congregation purchased the present church building from the American Lutheran Church which had been erected in 1956.

Through the years many pastors have served this congregation as it ministered and proclaimed Jesus Christ and Him crucified to the area of Redfield and the surrounding communities.

Faith Lutheran Church, Pierre, South Dakota

At the turn of the century missionaries of the Evangelical Lutheran Church of the Missouri Synod were ministering to the spiritual needs of Lutherans who had left larger congregations in the east and had come to a place where there was no church. There are no written records of the work at that time. According to oral reports, the little flock of Lutherans had a building of its own, and it was the "East Pierre Firehouse."

Because these people were interested in worshipping God they contacted the Reverend Walter Nitschke of Howard (who served at that time as the South Dakota District Mission Chairman), for services to be held in Pierre. Pastor Herman Bauer of Agar led the first worship services. Records also indicate that a Circuit Riding Pastor, Reverend Richard Schamber conducted worship services in Pierre shortly after the turn of the century.

Pastor Hugo Larson was ordained and installed as the first pastor of Faith Lutheran Church on September 6, 1931. History indicates that families from the Fairbanks Mission, northwest of Okoboji watched through the front store windows where Pastor Hugo Larson was being installed. Because they were Negro people they were not certain of their welcome with these Lutheran Christians at this time.

The parish held worship services in the Church of Christ just across from the present telephone building. Later they met in the St. Charles Hotel and the Courthouse.

The Fairbanks school mission, some 33 miles northwest of Pierre, was made up of families by the names of Speeces, William Day's children, Figgens, Harraway's children, and James McGruder and his mother, (who was affectionaly called Grandma). Grandma had no schooling and was perhaps 90 years old. In her youth before the end of the war she had witnessed the sale of a sister and brother at a slave auction in Hannibal, MO, never to see them again. When Pastor Larson once paid her a visit in her humble cottage, she held the Larson's oldest son and remarked that this was the first white child she had held in her arms since she was a slave some 65 years earlier.

By 1940 the congregation had grown to 75 communicant members and 47 baptized souls. Pastor R.H. Marquardt was now serving the church at Pierre.

In 1954 plans were made to either remodel the existing church or build a new one. The parish also decided at this time to become self-supporting. In 1958, property for the new church was purchased in the 700 block of North Grand. Plans were made to construct a new church which were finalized in 1960.

Groundbreaking ceremonies for the new church were held on March 19, 1961. By this time Faith Lutheran had grown to 327 communicant members and a total of 562 baptized members.

The present pastor, Pastor Brad Urbach, accepted the call to Faith and was installed in September of 1974. It was also time to think of adding to the building because of the growth of the congregation. Groundbreaking was held on June 25, 1978 and on Sunday December 3, 1978 the old mortgage was burned.

Additional property on Euclid Avenue was purchased in 1979 to accommodate the future expansion needs.

In the fall of 1979 Faith began a Christian pre-school. Kay Huksford was the first teacher/director. Janet Larson began in September 1986 and continues to serve as teacher/director today.

When some of the neighboring congregations became too small to support their pastor, Faith was approached to see whether they could supply staff to serve these small congregations. Faith was willing to call a second pastor who served Faith, Pierre as well as Trinity, Blunt and Immanuel, Harrold.

The congregation continually was active in serving the needs of the community of Pierre. In 1988 Faith Lutheran Day Care Center was opened with Sandra Hobart as teacher. This center cared for about 47 children from infancy through seven years old.

By the beginning of 1990, the membership of Faith totaled 1239 baptized souls and 892 communicant members. It was time once again to consider expansion of the building to meet the needs of the growing congregation. In September of 1995, the cornerstone was laid for the new worship facility with the framing and inside work proceeding rapidly through the winter months. In 1996, after the Ash Wednesday Service in the old sanctuary, the altar appointments were carried into the new facility. Members followed carrying their hymnals. The first Sunday worship service in the new sanctuary was held on February 25, 1996 with dedication day set for May 5, 1996.

The old sanctuary was then converted into a two-story education wing. This building now houses the pre-school as well as Day Care, storage and bathroom facilities. The newly poured second floor provides classrooms, a meeting room and a larger area for groups and games.

Faith Lutheran has for many years had a large and active youth group. The youth provided many activities for themselves as well as for children and members of the congregation. They have truly been a blessing to the congregation. The congregation, now over 70 years old, continues to serve God faithfully and minister to the people of the Pierre area in a large number of ways. Faith members have many reasons to be thankful to the Lord for His rich blessings over these 70 some years.

First English Lutheran Church, Centerville, South Dakota
Services have been held by pastors of the Lutheran Church – Missouri Synod in the community of Centerville since 1876. Most of these services were held in private homes in earlier years. However, in 1932 services began to be held in the city of Centerville.

It was at this time that Pastor H.H. Kuehn, pastor of Grace Lutheran Church (rural Centerville), found an opportunity to establish a mission in Centerville. When the Methodist-Episcopal church became vacant, Pastor Kuehn, trusting in the power of God, without any hope of financial aid, secured the use of this church for six months. Having done that, the Pastor personally cleaned the church, repaired the broken windows and bought a ton of coal. For the first few weeks Pastor Kuehn also served as his own janitor.

The first service was held on November 30, 1932 with a large number of worshippers present. Many were unknown to the pastor at that time.

In 1934 the congregation met to discuss the adoption of a constitution and the formal organization of the congregation. A second meeting was announced for December 4, 1934. At this meeting the constitution was adopted and signed by 11 charter members. The name chosen for the congregation was Our Savior Lutheran Church. This name was later changed to First English Lutheran Church.

By May of 1945 the members of First English Lutheran Church decided to buy the church building which they had been using up until this time. The building was purchased for $2,000. As the church continued to grow and the style of church was not in keeping with Lutheran art and architecture, it was decided to rebuild the church. This building project began in 1949. The first service was held in the new church on October 15, 1950. The members of First English worship in that same facility today.

Our Redeemer Lutheran Church, Custer, South Dakota

In the 1930's the South Dakota District of the LCMS was looking for a way to reach out with the Gospel in the areas of southwestern South Dakota. It was in 1935 that a call was extended to the Reverend R.W. Uecker to serve as Missionary-at-Large for this territory of the southern Black Hills. Pastor Uecker arrived in Custer on September 13, 1935 and was installed by the Reverend John Wild at the Junction Schoolhouse about seven or eight miles northwest of Custer on October 6, 1935. A place of worship was established at the White Church on the corner of 5th and Harney Streets for evening services. The first service was scheduled for October 27, 1935. To the surprise of many, 76 worshippers appeared for that service. Sunday School classes began on December 8, 1935.

Because of the growth of the congregation and the need for larger and more permanent worship space, the South Dakota District was asked to purchase the three lots at the corner of 8th and Harney Streets where Our Redeemer Lutheran is now located. Thus, Our Redeemer Lutheran Church was organized at a meeting held October 2, 1936. Groundbreaking was held and the basement was being dug.

Even though Our Redeemer was a new mission congregation, they were nevertheless mission-minded as they reached out to Christian people who needed their ministry in the Newcastle, Wyoming area as well as the Igloo, Provo, and Edgemont areas.

In June of 1946, another spot survey was held in Hill City which indicated that a number of people there desired that Lutheran services be started. So it was on June 30, 1946 that the first service was held at the White Church on top of the hill on the south end of Main Street. This building was used for about a year and a half and then services were moved to the community hall. Hill City and Custer were now being served as a dual parish and have been since 1946. Hill City and Custer still remain a dual parish today and serve the people with the Gospel of Jesus Christ in these areas of the southern Black Hills.

Grace Lutheran Church, Deadwood, South Dakota

It was in 1892 that Missionary F. Kiess, who served in the Mansfield, Lebanon and Ipswich areas, visited the Black Hills. He wrote that while South Dakota was a dry state, the Black Hills were definitely not. *"Saloons were the only place where men and women gathered to spend the time. The Saloon was usually the biggest building in town. We went to the Saloon to gather information and to meet people. The bartender was a congenial fellow and he invited all the people he met to the services to be held the following Sunday."*

Several Missionaries were sent to the Hills in the 1890's and early 1900's. One of these, the Reverend F. Pfotenhauer, stationed in Minneapolis, later became President of the Lutheran Church – Missouri Synod in 1911.

The church in Deadwood met in the City Hall through 1934 and then in 1935 moved to the Firemen's Hall. The Deadwood Mission became organized as Grace Lutheran Church on March 22, 1936 with 80 baptized members and 40 communicant members. The congregation was incorporated under the laws of the State of South Dakota on April 29, 1936.

On September 20, 1936 the congregation resolved to purchase a building site on upper Main Street. A building committee was appointed and, in January of 1937, work began. A parsonage and church basement were the first to be constructed. Dedication of the basement and first service was held on September 29,1940.

God continues to bless this congregation these many years as faithful pastors have served, bringing the water of life to the members of the Deadwood community!

St. John's Lutheran Church, Montrose, South Dakota

It was in 1939 that St. John's of Montrose had its beginning under the direction of Reverend A.C. Oberheu of Zion, Canistota. Pastor Oberheu gathered about 50 people for a worship service. Desiring a place to worship, the dilapidated Baptist church in Montrose was purchased from the American

Legion. After much work by the members of the congregation, the first worship service was held for 90 worshippers July 30, 1939. On October 8, 1939, St. John's Lutheran Church was dedicated to the service of the Lord and had grown to a congregation of 70, with thirty-eight communicants.

In September of 1950 the first resident Pastor, the Reverend A.G. Palecheck was installed.

As the congregation continued to grow, a basement, a new kitchen and an altar grouping were added between 1955 and 1962.

Through God's grace the church has continued to grow over these many years. Many dedicated people are involved in mission projects and in reaching out to the citizens of Montrose and throughout the world with their mission offerings and prayers that the Gospel of Jesus Christ might come to all people. Their motto has been and continues to be, "The Lord has done great things to us, wherefore we are glad."

St. Paul Lutheran Church, Spearfish, South Dakota

It was on March 29, 1925 that Pastor Benedict Schwarz of Zion congregation in Rapid City conducted a communion service at Spearfish with 15 people present.

In the early 1930's various preaching services were held in Spearfish, Aladdin, Sundance and the CCC Camps. St. Paul congregation was organized and the first services were held in the 7th Day Adventist Church on 5th Street on April 29, 1940. The first resident pastor was P.L. Friedrich who came in 1941.

St. Paul Lutheran Church, Spearfish, SD

On May 26, 1942, St. Paul Lutheran joined with the Lutheran Church – Missouri Synod at a District convention at Madison, South Dakota. The church body purchased three and one half lots on the corner of 7th Street and Illinois Avenue for the price of $2,000. Construction of the new church began in July of 1944.The church was built with almost entirely volunteer labor and was finished and dedicated on June 22, 1947.

Several years later a new parsonage was constructed on the church property. Eight years later a new and larger church was under construction at the corner of 7th Street and Kansas Avenue. This new church was dedicated on June 5, 1955 with the Reverend Philip Mueller, District President, delivering the Dedication Sermon.

At this time St. Paul Lutheran was also serving Mount Calvary Lutheran Church of Sundance, Wyoming. When Mount Calvary was granted a release from St. Paul, St. Paul's pastor began to serve the campus ministry at Black Hills State College. St. Paul congregation is served today by the Reverend Gene Bauman, 2nd Vice-President of the South Dakota District of the Lutheran Church – Missouri Synod.

God continues to shower his blessings upon the members of St. Paul as they reach out to the students on the college campus as well as the people of Spearfish.

Redeemer Lutheran Church, Clearfield, South Dakota

Redeemer, Clearfield SD - church and former parsonage

Redeemer Lutheran Church of Clearfield, South Dakota was organized as a congregation on October 30, 1940. Compared to other congregations, Redeemer is not very old. However, her history as a preaching station goes back to the days of homesteading. When homesteading was opened in this area of the state in 1909, many Lutherans settled in the area and were served by the Reverend H. Weertz of Naper, NE. Hope congregation, (15 miles south of Colome) and Jerusalem congregation (11 miles south of Carter) were organized. These two congregations formed a parish of some 800 square miles. At this time Clearfield served as a preaching station with services held in homes, schools, and a store building that once stood across the road from the present church.

It was during the ministry of Reverend Streufert that the preaching station of Clearfield became an organized congregation of the Lutheran Church – Missouri Synod. On October 30, 1940, seven men gathered at the home of Mr. and Mrs. Harry Ahlers for the purpose of organizing a congregation. They chose the name of Redeemer Lutheran Church, drew up, adopted and signed the constitution. Thus Redeemer Lutheran congregation was organized with seven voters, 17 communicants and 22 baptized souls. They purchased a school building, moved it to Clearfield and added on to it as they prepared to use it for a house of worship. When in 1953, the Jerusalem congregation disbanded (with some of the members joining the Wisconsin Synod congregations), Redeemer formed a dual parish with Trinity Lutheran Church of Dixon.

On March 15, 1957 the Dixon congregation was released of its parish obligations with Clearfield. It was decided that Redeemer and the Winner preaching station would issue a call for a pastor. On August 17, 1958 Candidate J. Wilk was installed as pastor of the Clearfield-Winner parish.

In the fall of 1972 discussion began regarding the formation of a 3-point parish, namely, Winner-Clearfield-Hamill, with the understanding that Hamill (which was an ALC congregation) would join the Lutheran Church – Missouri Synod.

God's rich blessing still attends the preaching of his word in this sparsely populated area of our state.

Redeemer Lutheran Church, Armour, South Dakota

The "mother" church of the Armour-Corsica parish was the former St. Paul's Evangelical Lutheran Church, located seven miles west and two miles south of Armour. The history of Redeemer Lutheran dates back to 1935. Pastor H.H. Stahnke, then serving St. Paul's Lutheran Church west of Armour and St. Peter's Lutheran Church in Corsica, began services in the town of Armour. In early 1941 a meeting was called in Redeemer Lutheran Church for the purpose of organizing a congregation. A constitution was drawn up and adopted and the congregation organized under the name of Redeemer Evangelical Lutheran Church of the Unaltered Augsburg Confession. At the time of organization the congregation numbered six voters, 28 communicants and 50 souls. The congregation rented the Episcopal church building until 1944, when it purchased the building, redecorated it inside and out and refurnished it with new pews and chairs. Gifts were given by various congregations around the area to assist the new congregation as it started its ministry. The church was dedicated to the glory of God on May 6, 1945 and incorporated in 1948 under the name of Redeemer Evangelical Lutheran Congregation. A youth group, ladies aid and men's group all began to organize in order to involve the people in the ministry of the congregation as well as fellowship with their fellow believers in Christ.

In September of 1947 Redeemer congregation voted to build a new parsonage at a cost of $13,000. In 1987 the parsonage was remodeled to better serve the needs of the pastor and his family.

As the years went by, it became apparent that a new and larger house of worship was needed. In 1953 the voters set a goal of three years for a new church building. And so it was on June 14, 1959 that the present house of worship was dedicated. In 1954 the St. Paul congregation was disbanded. The bell which used to hang in the tower of St. Paul's church now hangs in the tower of Redeemer Lutheran Church. May God's rich blessings continue to attend the members of Redeemer as they serve Him as his chosen people in the Armour community.

Our Savior Lutheran Church, Igloo, South Dakota

Records are sketchy on this congregation which is no longer in existence. Many of the records have been destroyed and so these notes were written down by one of the last pastors to have served there.

When the Black Hills Ordinance Depot was being built in 1942, the Reverend R.W. Uecker, visitor of the Rapid City Circuit, started services in the town of Edgemont, SD. These services were basically held for the workers of the construction crews. When the depot was opened later to residents and business, every church denomination wanted to hold services, but the government stated that only the churches that were conducting services in Edgemont would be permitted to come to Igloo. Thus it was that the Lutheran Church was permitted to have its early beginning in Igloo.

The first pastor to be called in 1943 was the Reverend Walldamore Thiele.

The congregation was officially accepted as a member of the Lutheran Church – Missouri Synod on June 1, 1945. According to a report of January 2, 1950, there were about 105 baptized members and 55 communicants. Since 1950 the congregation had grown to 279 baptized and 165 communicants.

In July of 1955, this congregation took upon itself the labor of love of starting services in the town of Edgemont. Because of various happenings with the railroad, this congregation has now closed.

Trinity Lutheran Church, Edgemont, South Dakota

Very little is recorded about the Trinity Lutheran congregation of Edgemont except what is noted in the Igloo congregation records.

Trinity of Edgemont was released from the South Dakota District of the Lutheran Church – Missouri Synod and accepted into membership with the South Dakota District of The American Lutheran Church by action of its convention on June 2, 1978.

Trinity Lutheran Church, Claire City, South Dakota

This once again is a congregation which has no records on file in the Archives at the District Office. We do know that this congregation disbanded because it had shrunk to the point that they could no longer function efficiently. Most of the members joined neighboring Missouri Synod congregations.

Memorial Lutheran Church, Sioux Falls, South Dakota

In March 1943 the Reverend P.R. Albrecht, Secretary of Missions for the South Dakota District of The Lutheran Church – Missouri Synod came to Sioux Falls to survey the possibility of starting a new congregation. Even though there were already three synodical conference churches in the city, there were many people who believed that, with the fast growth of Sioux Falls, a new congregation was needed in the northwest part of the city to accommodate people moving to that area.

Because the conditions proved favorable for the beginning of a new mission, the Board of Directors of the South Dakota District of the Lutheran Church – Missouri Synod sent a divine call to the Reverend Herman E. Rossow, a ministerial candidate at Concordia Seminary in St. Louis. Pastor Rossow accepted the call and arrived in Sioux Falls on August 13, 1943.

Now came the challenge for the new mission to find a suitable place of worship.

The South Dakota District purchased two lots at 11th Street and Willow Avenue in preparation for a church. Groundbreaking was held on May 24, 1944 and the excavation of the church basement began the following day.

The first service was held in the new basement on September 3, 1944 with 26 people in attendance. The congregation was officially organized and named Memorial Lutheran Church. The Reverend Herman E. Rossow was installed as the first pastor of the congregation on October 24, 1944.

Memorial Lutheran Church, Sioux Falls, SD new building 1999

Memorial Lutheran Church was officially dedicated to the service of the Lord on June 10, 1945.

At the annual meeting on January 2, 1946 the Voters' Assembly passed a resolution to assume ownership of the church building and property from the South Dakota District. Four days later the assembly passed a resolution to incorporate in accordance with state law and the articles of incorporation were filed with the Secretary of State on November 30, 1946.

As the congregation continued to grow, it was decided in February of 1951 that the congregation would begin to make plans to build a sanctuary above the basement. The structure was started in November 1953, completed in the spring of 1954 and dedicated on June 30, 1954. As the congregation continued to grow, a new addition was needed to meet the needs of the people. And so a new addition was added and dedicated on April 1, 1978.

Again, with the congregation's continued growth, a search for more space was begun. Need was felt to relocate to better serve the needs of the people of Sioux Falls. Thus it was on April 25, 1991 that the congregation voted to purchase approximately seven acres of land at 5000 South Western Avenue in Sioux Falls. The land was dedicated at a special service at the site in September of 1991.

Today, Memorial worships in a new facility at 5000 South Western Avenue serving the needs of a growing congregation. May God's rich blessings continue to attend these Lutheran Christians.

Our Savior Lutheran Church, Aberdeen, South Dakota

It was in September of 1946 that our South Dakota District Mission Board, following a survey and many discussions, decided to establish a "preaching station" on the north side of Aberdeen. This preaching station is now known as Our Savior Lutheran Church. This early church held services in the Monroe School with Pastor A. Bartels as first pastor.

On March 9, 1947 the congregation was officially organized. The signing of the Constitution occurred on July 13th. A Sunday School was organized in September of 1946 and a Ladies Aid in November of 1946.

As membership and attendance grew, the Monroe School Library and Music Room were unable to hold the numbers of people for Sunday Services, so it was at this time that plans were drawn and six lots were purchased at the corner of North Jay and 7th Avenue NE for the construction of a new building for the cost of $1,900. The basement was completed on November 6, 1949 at the approximate cost of $25,000. This basement was used for the church for several years, giving the congregation time to gather funds for the next phase of its structure.

Following Pastor Bartels was Pastor Ralph Wegner who served as vacancy pastor until August of 1949 when Pastor Harvey Kreuger was installed as pastor. Under Pastor Kreuger's direction Our Savior was to continue its rapid growth as the basement was soon bursting at the seams.

A formal youth program was started in 1950 with the formation of the Walther League.

Following Pastor Kreuger's ministry was that of Pastor Edgar Struefert who served as vacancy pastor until November of 1953 when Pastor Marxson Dommer was installed. It was at this time that the Voters' Assembly decided to draw plans for a church structure to better serve their needs. On July 12, 1955 groundbreaking began to enlarge the basement and build a superstructure. The cost of this superstructure was $150,000 which included grounds, buildings and furnishings.

A very special event in the life of the congregation occurred on February 13, 1955. Pastor Dommer said to the congregation; "One of the greatest privileges of my life came to me last Sunday when I had the distinct honor of baptizing 24 children in a mass children's baptism service – a day long to be remembered."

On October 9, 1955 the cornerstone was laid and on July 1, 1956 members gathered for the unlocking of the doors and the dedication of the newly completed superstructure. Various services of praise and thanksgiving were offered God for this special celebration and for his rich blessings upon the congregation.

By the time Pastor Dommer accepted a call and left Our Savior congregation in January of 1959, the congregation had grown to 714 baptized and 425 communicant members.

The congregation then was served by Pastor Alva F. Pingel, followed by Pastor Raymond Pomplun. Following Pastor Pomplun, Pastor Terry Naasz, (presently pastor at Mount Calvary in Brookings) served the congregation for a number of years. The present pastors are Reverend John Farden and Pastor Jais Tinglund. Recently, a fellowship hall has been added to the building.

God continues His rich blessings upon the members of Our Savior as they remain faithful to Him in proclaiming His precious Gospel to a world so much in need.

Concordia Lutheran Church, Cresbard, South Dakota

Services were begun in a schoolhouse seven miles north of Cresbard on October 10, 1937 by Pastor W.A. Bunkowske of Wecota. These services continued for two years. On November 8, 1940 services and Sunday school were started at Cresbard at the Congregational Church. This terminated in April 1941 when Reverend Bunkowske accepted a call to Waubay, South Dakota.

In the fall of 1942, Reverend David J.O. Loesch accepted the call to Immanuel Lutheran, Wecota. In this call he was directed to do mission work in Cresbard. Services were begun February 23, 1947 in the Methodist Church and on April 13, 1947 the first service was held in the Congregational Church.

At a meeting on March 15, 1948, the church was officially organized with a constitution and the name "Concordia Evangelical Lutheran Church" adopted.

Incorporation took place October 8, 1961. The Congregational Church, Cresbard was used in 1940-1941 and again beginning January 4, 1948, and purchased in March, 1950 for $1,500. On January 26, 1960, it was decided to build for approximately $50,000. Lots were purchased adjacent to the Immanuel Lutheran Church, Wecota's parsonage (which is in the town of Cresbard).

Groundbreaking services were held on the church site on September 15, 1963. Building operations began September 16, 1963 and the cornerstone laid October 20, 1963. Dedication of this new church was held on Pentecost Sunday, May 17, 1964.

Concordia Lutheran Church, Vermillion, SD

For many years the vision remained in the minds of many that a Missouri Synod Lutheran Church needed to be established in the city of Vermillion. So it was in the early 1940's that the "Lewis House", a familiar landmark to early residents and now an apartment house on Cottage Avenue was acquired to serve as a chapel and parsonage for a new congregation. Services during those early years were conducted sporadically by neighboring pastors. In 1947, the Reverend W. P. Haak of Yankton was appointed to supervise the development in Vermillion. A handful of students and local residents were gathered together for worship in the Odd Fellows Hall.

At the beginning of 1948, the District resolved to call a Candidate for the purpose of building a local congregation and contacting students at the University of South Dakota. Ralph L. Moellering, a 1946 graduate of Concordia Seminary, St. Louis, (at that time an instructor at Concordia Teacher's College in Seward, NE) was called. Concordia was adopted as the permanent name for the congregation to signify the doctrinal harmony and peaceful relations upon which it was founded.

On April 17, 1949 a meeting was held, at which time a constitution was adopted and the congregation was officially organized.

At the 1951 South Dakota District Convention at Freeman, SD, the decision was made to move ahead as rapidly as possible with the construction of a church in Vermillion. Early in 1952, bids were received on the sale of the "Lewis House." Plans for a new chapel and student center were presented and adopted. Excavation began in April.

The first services in the new building were held during the Christmas season of 1952. The new church building (which still serves the community) was dedicated on April 19, 1953. The total cost of the building was $97,584.

Just how many lives have been touched by the grace of God and the love of Jesus Christ at Concordia, only God knows. We certainly pray God's continued blessings upon the members of Concordia as they minister to the students at the University of South Dakota as well as the members of the Vermillion community.

Concordia Lutheran Church, Wessington, South Dakota

On December 10, 1950, a small group of Lutheran families in and around Wessington held their first church services in what was known as the Old German Lutheran Church building. This building was then used by the Church of Christ members. Pastor David Loesch conducted these services. A Sunday School was also started at this time.

During the early months of 1951, the services were held at the Edward Neilsen home until arrangements could be made to have services on Sunday afternoon at the Church of Christ building.

Early in 1951, the members decided to buy the Peace Lutheran Church from Virgil, South Dakota. The church was moved from Virgil to Wessington, remodeled and painted for their church home.

On September 2, 1951 a groundbreaking service was held on a lot donated by Mr. Emil Martens. The name selected in 1952 for the church was Concordia Lutheran.

On September 2, 1952 the church was dedicated to the praise and honor of God for His guidance and protection in giving them this place of worship.

It was on October 6, 1991 when the congregation celebrated its 40th anniversary as well as the dedication of a new fellowship hall, new kitchen and bathroom that were placed all on one level.

In 1992 Concordia established a Lutheran pre-school under the direction of Mrs. Ruth Rynearson of Wolsey. Classes began with 20 students. The pre-school continues to serve the community to this present day.

On January 1, 2000 a new parish agreement with Concordia of Wessington, Zion of Wessington Springs and Mount Olive of Woonsocket was established and became known as a three-point parish called Peace Lutheran Rural Parish.

Bethlehem Lutheran Church, Rapid City, South Dakota

Bethlehem congregation began under God's blessings in 1948 when Pastor R.W. Uecker of Our Redeemer Lutheran Church in Custer and Reverend R.H. Marquardt of Zion Lutheran Church in Rapid City did a preliminary canvass of the Canyon Lake Area of Rapid City in order to determine the feasibility of starting a congregation in that area. Potential was recognized and the South Dakota District of The Lutheran Church – Missouri Synod agreed to open a new mission station in the Canyon Lake Area of Rapid City.

The Reverend Floyd Schweiger of Ft. Wayne, Indiana accepted the District's call to be "Missionary-at-Large" for this new venture. He came in "the blizzard of 1949." Pastor Schweiger canvassed the area and found adequate interest to start worship services. They were to meet in the shelter at Canyon Lake Park but had to wait until the weather warmed in order to do so. In March of 1949 eight lots on Rushmore Street, including a small house which would be used as a parsonage, was purchased from the Rushmore Life Insurance Company at the cost of $5,028. Four adjacent lots were purchased in 1951 for $600 each. Plans were made for the purchase of a portable chapel from Portland, Oregon. This chapel would remain the property of the District to be used in other places after a permanent building was built.

The first worship service was announced for April 24, 1949. A total of 13 people were present for the service at the Shelter House at Canyon Lake Park and seven children attended Sunday School. The portable chapel arrived in June of 1949 and was constructed in what is now the church parking lot by volunteers. VBS was held, which was a stepping stone for evangelism and congregation-building. The first service in this chapel was held in July of 1949 even before it was completed. The congregation was then officially organized on November 22, 1950. Several members from Zion Lutheran came over to help with the start of the new congregation, keeping their membership at Zion. Soon thereafter a Women's Guild, associated with the Lutheran

Women's Missionary League was started as well as a youth group known as the Walther League, which attracted people also from the community. Following Pastor Schweiger's ministry, the Reverend Arthur Crosmer of Powell, Wyoming (later to become District President) came as pastor to Bethlehem. An addition was added to the parsonage to accommodate Pastor Crosmer's family, which included four children. In May of 1958 the District deeded the church property to Bethlehem Lutheran Church for $24,669.41.

It was now time for a new permanent church building. The building debt of $92,447.83 (financed by a commercial loan and later by a Church Extension Fund loan) seemed out of sight for this small flock worshipping at this time, however, God had different plans. Groundbreaking was held for the new building on Pentecost Sunday, May 17, 1959 with cornerstone laying on August 30, 1959 and church dedication on December 8, 1959.

In February of 1970 Pastor Crosmer accepted the call to become President of the South Dakota District and the Reverend Herb Schultze was called to be pastor.

In June of 1972 Rapid City and Bethlehem Lutheran were traumatized by a killer flood. One life from the congregation's membership was lost and many families suffered property damage. Following Pastor Schultze's term of office, Pastor Allen Jacobson came to serve Bethlehem. The time came to add to the church structure in order for the congregation to meet its meeting, Sunday School, etc., requirements. The last payment of the original church building debt was made in May of 1988 and a special mortgage-burning ceremony was held on September 11, 1988.

Following Pastor Jacobson's pastorate, the Reverend Vernon L. Schindler, current President of the South Dakota District LCMS, became pastor of Bethlehem. He was installed on April 16, 1989. Having been a former missionary in Ghana, Pastor Schindler was able to share much from the mission field as well as inviting missionaries in to share their experiences with the congregation and heighten the awareness of the mission work that we are doing throughout the world. A year following Pastor Schindler's installation, it was time for the much-needed addition to the church building. This addition included a reception area, classroom space, fellowship hall, meeting space and upstairs restrooms. This addition was dedicated to the Lord's work on November 21, 1991. Building cost financed by AAL was $220,000.

In 1996 the congregation purchased the house and land across Rushmore Street from the church to be used as a residence for vicars and additional parking for Sunday services.

Several vicars have served Bethlehem the past years. Present pastor is Reverend William Paepke.

Chapter 12
The Last 55 years-

Our Savior's Lutheran Church, Hill City, South Dakota

Our Savior Lutheran Church, Hill City

The first service of Our Savior's Lutheran Church in Hill City was conducted on June 30, 1946 by Reverend R.W. Uecker. Incorporation of the congregation was documented on August 10, 1952. A variety of locations were utilized for services, including the Little White Church, until the church in its present location could be built. The basement was dedicated in December, 1962. First services in the basement sanctuary were held in the fall of 1963. Dedication of the present sanctuary over the basement occurred in January, 1976, and the mortgage was burned January 28, 1990. Since that time the stained glass windows were installed and the sanctuary was made completely handicapped accessible. Through these many years God has blessed Our Savior's congregation with dedicated, capable servants, ordained as well as lay.

Holy Cross Lutheran Church, Onida, South Dakota

Having traveled to Agar to attend church services for a number of years, a group of Missouri Synod Lutherans from Onida decided it was time to conduct services in their town on an experimental basis. The first service was held July 8,1951 in the basement of the city auditorium with 35 people in attendance. When the members of the Methodist church heard that they were worshipping in the auditorium, they graciously offered the use of their building for a rental fee of $10/month.

Two months later Holy Cross Lutheran Church was organized on September 14, 1951. A constitution was drawn up to serve the new congregation. A loan was sought from the Church Extension Fund to pay for the property at the present church site. This property was purchased for $4,000.

In 1952 Pastor O.D. Brack, (from Gettysburg) located an unused congregational church building near Tolstoy. This building was purchased for $1,700 and moved to Onida to serve as their church home. Following some remodeling, the church was dedicated on March 30, 1955. As the congregation continued to grow, an educational unit was proposed for the growing Sunday school as well as the pastor's office. Groundbreaking ceremonies were held in October of 1965 and the dedication was held March 13, 1966. God's rich blessings have attended Holy Cross these past years. It is with that same confidence that they look forward to the future to His continued grace and blessings.

Our Redeemer Lutheran Church, Sioux Falls, South Dakota

Seeing a need for a church in (what was at that time) western Sioux Falls, the South Dakota District purchased a plot of land at Western Avenue and Oak Street. Two years later, in June of 1954, a temporary chapel was completed. Vacation Bible School was held under the direction of Chaplain Carl Tubesing of the Veteran's Hospital. On September 27, 1954 the Chapel was dedicated and the Reverend Norbert A. Streufert was installed as the first pastor. In October of 1954, the constitution and bylaws of the congregation were adopted.

Following Pastor Streufert's ministry Pastor Russell Grundmeier was installed as pastor of Our Redeemer in January of 1960. (Pastor Grundmeier is still a member of Our Redeemer, living in eastern Sioux Falls in his retirement years.)

By August 13, 1961 the church was ready to have its groundbreaking services for the new facility. The cornerstone was laid in a special service on July 1, 1962. Much of the interior finish work of the church was done by volunteer labor from the congregation. It was on Sunday, September 9, 1962 that Our Redeemer Lutheran Church dedicated its new house of worship. The first chapel was then converted to a parsonage.

Our Redeemer Lutheran Church, Sioux Falls SD

The church continued to grow. Since the congregation had been on mission status and subsidized by the District from 1954 through 1965, the voters determined that District support was no longer necessary, so they became self-supporting that year. It was now time to think of further building structure to meet the needs of the growing congregation. And so some work in remodeling the kitchen of the parsonage and an educational unit addition to the church were in the making. This new education addition was begun on May 15, 1975. On February 15, 1976, the education unit was complete and dedication ceremonies were conducted.

Now it was time to become involved in another ministry – namely that of Christian Education. In July of 1976 a resolution was made to establish a Lutheran School in association with other Missouri Synod congregations in Sioux Falls. On April 24, 1977 the voters approved the use of Our Redeemer's educational facilities by the Sioux Falls Lutheran School Association. The Reverend George Sagissor presently serves as pastor to the members of the congregation.

Redeemer Lutheran Church, Iroquois, South Dakota

It was on March 14, 1954 that the first sermon was preached to members who were to become Redeemer Lutheran Church of Iroquois, South Dakota.

Sixty-five people assembled for that first service led by the Reverend Willard Koch of Yale, South Dakota. Crude pews on the ground floor of an old assembly building known as the Old Opera House were in place for the first service. It was the climax of a great deal of labor and the realization of a fervent hope of many people.

Use of the Old Opera House had been obtained for a rent of $10/month from the Odd Fellows Lodge, which was using the second floor of the rather dilapidated building for its meeting place. The spacious first floor with its gymnasium floor and roomy stage was readied for holding of worship services by the new congregation.

Opening day found 65 people attending the opening service. An estimated 250 people attended the open house event in the evening.

Nineteen days later on Friday, March 2, a group of 14 men gathered in the chapel for the purpose of discussing the matter of organizing a congregation. A tentative constitution was drafted and on May 16 the committee's work was presented to the prospective voters. Articles of Incorporation and a constitution were studied and adopted. In May a request was made of the District convention to accept this new congregation as a member of the Lutheran Church – Missouri Synod.

With the adoption of a constitution and thereby organizing into a congregation, the Iroquois mission became Redeemer Lutheran Church. Reverend Willard Koch of Yale was called to serve them as an additional charge to his parish in Yale.

Only slightly more than a year after services were begun in Iroquois, the congregation was offered a church building of a disbanded sister congregation in James, South Dakota for the price of $1,000. But God had different plans. The final decision for moving the building was to be made on May 2, 1955, but before that date they heard the tragic news that fire had destroyed the church building which they had intended to purchase.

So disappointment was evident for these people, yet God had even better plans in mind. Peace congregation in Virgil, South Dakota was considering disbanding and selling their church building. This new Redeemer congregation was given the first opportunity to purchase the building. March 7th, one week before its second birthday, Redeemer congregation, in a special meeting, agreed to purchase the Peace Lutheran Church building for $2,500, (provided that it would be feasible to move it to Iroquois). On June 7, 1956 lots were purchased for a home for the new building. Groundbreaking ceremonies were held on June 13.

Due to dwindling membership, the congregation was forced to disband in May of 1995. Even though their time of service was short, only eternity will tell the number of souls that were touched by the ministry held in that place.

Christ Lutheran Church, Sioux Falls, South Dakota

It was late 1955 that the South Dakota District of the Lutheran Church – Missouri Synod's mission board began investigating the need for a congregation in the Hilltop Heights area of Sioux Falls. Such a need did exist and Pastor Karl Paul of Memorial Lutheran Church in Sioux Falls was asked to begin work in that area.

The first service (together with Sunday School) was held on February 19, 1956 in the Edwin Bader residence at 3205 East 17th Street. From that time on, Pastor Paul led worship services on Sunday afternoons.

It was with great rejoicing that on October 14, 1956 the first resident pastor, the Reverend Paul G. Wendling was installed. (Pastor Wendling later became our District President). A parsonage was purchased at 2412 East 19th Street and the basement was readied for use as a place to hold worship services. Used chancel furniture was given by Our Savior Lutheran Church in Aberdeen. On November 18, 1956 worship services and Sunday School were conducted in the parsonage basement.

As the congregation grew, property needed to be purchased for a permanent site for the new congregation. So the South Dakota District purchased property at 15th Street and Cleveland Avenue and was granted a loan from the CEF to begin work on a building.

Ground was broken for the new church on March 10, 1957 with cornerstone-laying on May 5, 1957.

On April 17, 1957 Christ Lutheran Church was formally organized with 12 charter members signing the constitution. The congregation became a member of the South Dakota District of the Lutheran Church – Missouri Synod the following month.

The new church was dedicated on August 18, 1957 and was made up of 14 families (32 communicant members).

Since the congregation did not have large sums of money, it was left to various members of the congregation to build furniture such as the altar, pulpit, lectern, baptismal font, communion rail, candelabra, flower stands, outside bulletin board and speaker box, and lighted cross above the altar. These chancel furnishings were dedicated on June 11, 1961.

Following six years of shepherding by Pastor Wendling, Pastor Clemens E. Harms was installed as new pastor of Christ Lutheran.

On January 1, 1970 the voters agreed that, as of that date, Christ Lutheran would become a self-sustaining congregation.

In the early 1970's Pastor Harms began to talk of a need for a Lutheran School in Sioux Falls. His dream was that the other LCMS congregations in Sioux Falls would join in such a venture. And so it was on May 22, 1977 that Christ voters adopted a resolution committing themselves to membership in the Sioux Falls Lutheran School Association. Five Missouri Synod churches of Sioux Falls joined to form that Association on October 12, 1977.

President Vernon Schindler served as pastor at Christ Lutheran from 1984-1989. In the early 1990's the District saw the need for a possible mission site on the far east side of Sioux Falls. Land was purchased on 6th Avenue for a possible church site.

There was a need at that time for better facilities for Siouxland Lutheran Church for the Deaf. When talk began about building something for the deaf, Christ approached the District Board to find out whether they could be the new mission church together with the Deaf church in that area of town. So in 1995 a building was ready for Christ Lutheran Church and a Chapel for Trinity Lutheran Church for the Deaf. Having both the deaf and hearing congregations together has done much to encourage the understanding of needs of fellow Christians.

We pray God's blessings upon this venture and these people of God in the future as He has so bountifully blessed them in the past.

Christ Lutheran Church, Winner, South Dakota

In the early 1950's the need was showing itself for a Missouri Synod Lutheran Church in the Winner area. So on December of 1956, Pastor Walter Klipp of Chamberlain held a service for interested Lutherans at the home of John and Marie Weidner.

A mission preaching station was set up and, during the first few months of 1957, worship services were held in the Legion Club with Pastor Klipp, Pastor S.J. Lehmann of Gregory and Pastor D.S. Sallach of Fairfax preaching.

In March of 1957, Redeemer of Clearfield and the preaching station in Winner elected to call a pastor to serve both congregations.

In June of 1957 the purchase of three corner lots in Winner occurred, providing a place for a new church to be built.

In October of the same year, the name of Christ Lutheran Church was chosen for this new congregation. They applied for membership in the Lutheran Church – Missouri Synod and signed the constitution which was adopted on June 17, 1958.

On August 17, 1958 Candidate James L. Wilk was ordained and installed as the first resident pastor of Christ Lutheran Church.

With great rejoicing, Christ Lutheran was accepted as a congregation of the Missouri Synod Lutheran Church at the convention in Sioux Falls on September 24, 1958.

The time had come for a new structure to be built. On May 3, 1959, the groundbreaking ceremonies were held and construction began shortly thereafter. The cornerstone was laid in August of 1959. The first services were held in the basement of the new church on the first Sunday after Thanksgiving in 1959. Christmas Eve and Christmas Day services were the first services held in the new sanctuary. The new church was dedicated on January 10, 1960.

It was in 1968 that the members of Christ Lutheran indicated an interest in making an outreach to the Indian people of Winner. A canvass of the Indian community resulted in 37 children of Indian background who attended VBS in the summer of 1969.

In the fall of 1972, discussions began regarding formation of a three-point parish (Winner-Clearfield-Hamill) with the understanding that the Hamill congregation (ALC) would join the Missouri Synod. And so on January 13, the Voters' Assembly approved of entering into a three-point parish structure with Hamill and Clearfield.

As members continue to come and go, the Gospel message spreads even to the far corners of the earth.

Faith Lutheran Church, Parkston, South Dakota

Early in 1956 a group of people believed it was time to form a Missouri Synod Lutheran Church in the Parkston area. With 15 people in attendance, a meeting was held on August 23, 1956 to express their needs, wants and desires to form a church and fulfill a dream. With the help of Pastor James Hawley of Tripp and the South Dakota District, this dream became a reality.

The first concern was finding a place for worship. The old County Building was to be where the first service was held on October 7, 1956. As more and more people joined the membership of this new congregation, God moved Mr. and Mrs. Schumacher to offer the church some land as a gift for a building site. A basement church was built at a cost of $9,000 and dedicated on July 21, 1957.

God continued to bless this little flock as it continued in growth and so the basement was enlarged and a church was built over the top. The finished structure was dedicated on October 1, 1961, with a final cost of $40,000 (complete with furnishings).

On January 26, 1975 the congregation decided it was time for its own pastor. Pastor August C. Roessler became the first called pastor of Faith.

That same year the church built a parsonage and dedicated it on September 14, 1975.

Once again as the church grew, there was a need for a building expansion. And so in January 1989 things began to move toward the construction of an expansion on the west side of the church. This new addition was dedicated on January 27, 1991. Over the years, Faith Lutheran has been served by a number of pastors. The present pastor is the Reverend Kenneth Soyk.

Mount Olive Lutheran Church, Watertown, South Dakota

Mount Olive Lutheran Church of Watertown, South Dakota was organized in October of 1956, under the leadership of Pastor J.G. Steinmeyer. Pastor Steinmeyer had been called by the District Mission Board in May of that year and was now called by Mount Olive congregation as its pastor. He was installed in the spring of 1957. Services for the new mission were held in the 1st Federal Savings and Loan building in Watertown until a structure was erected.

Land was purchased at 700 North Maple, and on October 16, 1966 groundbreaking for a new worship facility/educational wing took place. Rev. Ralph Mueller, Pastor of Mount Olive led the assembled congregation in worship.

On September 17, 1968 Pastor Roger Fisher dedicated the newly-built chapel and educational unit in a special service with President E.O. Luessenhop preaching.

Mount Olive Lutheran Church, Watertown, SD

The need soon became apparent for new and larger facilities for the ever-growing congregation and so a new church worship center with offices, etc. was built and dedicated on June 16, 1991. Pastor Robert Westad was serving as pastor at this time.

May God continue to shower His blessings upon His people in this place!

Our Savior's Lutheran Church, Springfield, South Dakota

For many years Lutherans in the Springfield vicinity desired a church home for their worship and praise of their Lord. Early services were held for the students at Southern State Teachers Colleges as well as evening services in the Episcopal church for members of the community.

Our Savior's, Springfield Xristos House Student Center (now closed)

In March 1956, regular services were held beginning with the first Sunday after Easter by Pastor D.E. Benson. Our Savior's Lutheran Chapel held its meetings in the Springfield Community Center until October 14, 1956.

Our Savior's Lutheran Church, Springfield, SD 1981

On July 27, 1956, a constitution and bylaws were drawn up and accepted by the new congregation. With assistance from the Mission Board of the South

Dakota District, a building was erected to be called Our Savior's Lutheran Chapel. When the student center was built by the District in Springfield, the pastor served the members of Our Savior's Lutheran Chapel as well as the students from the college who lived in the Student Center. Later it became necessary to close the student center because of the low number of students and financial burden of the ministry.

God continues to shower His blessings on this, his little flock in Springfield!

Our Savior Lutheran Church, Madison, South Dakota

It was on January 18, 1957 that a number of people formed Our Savior Lutheran Church in Madison and accepted a proposed constitution. The formation of this congregation happened to a large degree, because of the mission-mindedness of the people of St. Peter's Lutheran Church in Wentworth.

In 1956, the South Dakota District Mission Board felt it advisable to have a separate house of worship for the new congregation. Lots were purchased on the corner of 5th and Union and, following the construction of a basement, a church building was purchased from Mount Calvary Lutheran Church in Huron and moved to Madison.

Our Savior congregation has always felt a special mission to reach out to the students of Dakota State. A beautiful and well-equipped student center, complete with fireplace and kitchen facilities was incorporated into the design of the new building, and remains available for the students use during the academic year. The pastor is available to meet individually with students at any time. He spends time each week on campus visiting students.

In 1986, because of the greatly increased enrollment in Sunday School, the congregation decided to build additional classrooms onto the facilities. These classrooms were dedicated on January 18, 1987.

As indicated in their history on file in the District Office, these words apply well yet today, "...we have experienced the grace of God. He has showered blessing upon blessing upon us. To God alone be all glory and honor!"

Trinity Lutheran Church, Blunt, South Dakota

At a meeting at Blunt, South Dakota on November 25, 1962, twenty-one people representing 66 souls decided to work for organization of a congregation there.

The first worship service was held on December 16, 1962 in the American Legion Hall with 62 people in attendance. Pastor D.L. Gesterling of Harrold conducted the service. Later services were moved to the community room of the Rural Electric Power Building. In January of 1964, several lots were purchased in the north central part of town for a future building site.

In June of 1965, Lay Minister Leroy Glinsman came to serve Trinity of Blunt (together with Immanuel of Harrold) under the supervision of Pastor Hackbarth of Onida. Groundbreaking for a new church was held on October 3, 1965 with dedication services on May 22, 1966. Following Mr. Glinsman's service to the congregation was Lay Minister Edwin Bohnsack who came in 1973. Lay Minister Ray Rush then came and served Trinity beginning in 1977.

As it became ever more difficult to find pastoral leadership for these small congregations, some of the neighboring congregations offered assistance in serving them on a more or less permanent basis. So it was that Faith Lutheran Church of Pierre began serving the little flock at Blunt, as it does yet to this day.

Good Shepherd Lutheran Church, Ipswich, South Dakota

Good Shepherd Lutheran of Ipswich had its beginnings on Easter Sunday, April 14, 1963. Pastor Alva Pingel of Our Savior congregation in Aberdeen preached to the first worshippers in the Ipswich Legion Hall.

The first resident pastor of Good Shepherd was the Reverend Richard Brauer. It was during Pastor Brauer's pastorate that land was purchased for a church building which still serves the congregation to this day.

Groundbreaking for the new church building began in 1965, and in the fall of that year construction began. It was indeed a joyous occasion when on February 27, 1966 the members of Good Shepherd gathered for the first time in their new church to sing the praises of their Lord and King! The building was dedicated on April 24, 1966.

In 1967, Good Shepherd formed a parish with St. Paul's congregation of Leola. Various pastors served this new parish, including the Reverend Raymond Hartwig, (former District President and now serving as Secretary of The Lutheran Church – Missouri Synod). God's continued blessing rests upon this congregation as they serve the people of Ipswich.

Our Savior's Lutheran Church, Wilmot, South Dakota

It was in 1967 that Christ Lutheran Church and Centennial Lutheran church merged into one congregation.

The Reverend Fred Eberbach was pastor when the new church was formed in a parish with Bethlehem, rural Milbank. In 1978 Our Savior concluded their agreement with Bethlehem and aligned with Trinity congregation of Corona. This arrangement is still in operation today. All praise and glory to God for the message of salvation that is being proclaimed to the people of the Wilmot community by the pastor and people of Our Savior's!

Our Savior's Lutheran Church, Wilmot, SD

Peace Lutheran Church, Rapid City, South Dakota

The idea of starting a church in the south part of Rapid City was around for some time but it is difficult to establish an exact date for the beginning of (what was then) St. Luke Lutheran Church. Following canvassing by Vicar Wilbar Koehler in 1952, Zion Lutheran of Rapid City assembled a committee to check on the availability of a site. In 1953 this committee purchased a site at the corner of East Saint Anne and Maple streets.

The Mission Board then granted permission for Zion Lutheran to form a committee that would be responsible for the building. Construction began in February of 1954.

In June of 1954 the District called Candidate Donald R. Hoger as Missionary-at-Large in this area of Rapid City. Early notes indicate that Candidate Hoger was a "city boy" born and raised in Chicago. He couldn't drive a car. It was rather frightening to ride with him, but he did learn. The original building was an A-frame which cost $12,000 and the two lots $2,400. Later this building was torn down and a parking lot was put in this area when the new church was built.

That building was dedicated on August 15, 1954, with Sunday Services and Sunday School beginning August 22, 1954.

Peace Lutheran Church, Rapid City, SD

By 1959 the church had outgrown its building. Additional land was purchased across the alley from the church. So it was on March 7, 1965 that St. Luke congregation dedicated the new church building to the service and glory of God.

To go back to 1958, the South Dakota District purchased 10 acres in the northeast part of the city. Pastor E.C. Jones was called as Missionary-at-Large for a new mission station in that area of the city. First services were held October 9, 1960 in the basement of the newly-constructed parsonage. This mission station, named Ascension Lutheran Church, was to minister to the Native Americans as well as all people in the area. The first unit of the church was dedicated on July 9, 1961.

Although this mission field was not overly successful in gaining Native American members, it did grow. A second unit of Ascension was dedicated to God's glory on August 6, 1967.

In March 1970 a special "study group" was formed with St. Luke to study the feasibility of a joint or dual parish. A few months later, three members from Ascension and three members from St. Luke were appointed as a committee to work on the consolidation of the two congregations. So it was on August 16, 1970 that these two congregations approved the "plan of consolidation" and Peace Lutheran Church was born.

The facilities of St. Luke Lutheran Church were to be used by the new congregation. The first worship service as Peace Lutheran was held on June 7, 1970, although consolidation was not official until August 16, 1970.

As Peace continued to grow under God's blessings, there arose a need for additional space and on October 3, 1976 a fellowship hall and eight Sunday School classrooms were dedicated to the Lord. The A-frame that had been used for Sunday School and other activities was torn down.

Peace saw the need for a pre-school and, in July of 1988, a committee was appointed to establish the same. On June 18, 1989 the congregation authorized the starting of a pre-school and in September of 1989 it opened with 14 four-year-olds and 12 three-year-olds. Mrs. Shirley Wieman was the school's first director/teacher.

Expansion and remodeling of the chancel was again the order of the day. This was accomplished in 1994. The old communion railing was removed and reused with some new railing added and kneeling benches added in front of the chancel area on the same level as the nave. This more than doubled the number of communicants that could commune at the table at the same time. New carpeting was installed in the chancel and down the aisles.

As a colorful history unfolds for the members of Peace Lutheran Church, God's grace and rich blessings accompany them every step of the way!

Divine Shepherd Lutheran Church, Black Hawk, South Dakota

Near the end of 1984, the Board of Elders of Zion Lutheran Church, Rapid City, prompted by Zion's pastor, the Reverend Raymond L. Hartwig, discussed conducting a feasibility study for a new church start in the greater Rapid City area. In the spirit of our Lord's Great Commission, the Board was granted a go ahead by the Voters' Assembly to conduct such a study beginning in early January of 1985.

Following a lot of study of the Rapid City area and growth patterns of the same, three sites were chosen as possibilities for a mission, namely: "Sheridan Lake Road Area (SW); Mall Ridge Area (North) and the Black Hawk area (NW). By April of 1985 the committee members concluded that due to the population density, growth patterns on church statistics and lack of other denominational presence, the community of Black Hawk should be the area of interest for a mission start activity." So a preaching station in the Black Hawk community was recommended to Zion's Voters' Assembly. It was to begin in the fall of 1985, with a special effort being made to solicit the help and support of Zion members living in that community. Zion's voters unanimously accepted the proposal of the committee.

Now a place was needed for worship. It took no small amount of effort to locate one. The Rapid City School District finally agreed to set aside its building use regulations in order to permit regular use of the Black Hawk Elementary School gymnasium at a cost of $50 per Sunday. The first service and Sunday School of the Black Hawk preaching station was held on October 13, 1985 with 64 persons in attendance. As the small flock began to grow, a first adult instruction class and youth confirmation class were begun, holy communion under the auspices of Zion Lutheran was celebrated and the South Dakota District, LCMS was petitioned for help with the actual goal of a congregation being formed in Black Hawk.

The need for a building in which to continue meeting presented itself. It was decided that a multi-purpose structure be constructed of pre-engineered steel by SECO Construction of Rapid City. The estimated cost was to be approximately $150,000. A 2.3 acre parcel of land was located at the corner of Peaceful Pines Road and Wedgewood Street in Black Hawk. This land purchase, as well as a portion of the building cost, was financed by a grant from Forward In Remembrance. Ground for the new building was broken on August 3, 1986. The building was ready for occupancy by February 1, 1987.

The need for pastoral services had to be addressed. The pastors of Zion could not continue to serve the new congregation as it grew. When Zion's assistant pastor accepted a call, the South Dakota District Board of Directors acknowledged the promise of the beginnings of this new congregation and voted in November of 1986 to extend a call to Reverend Lloyd Redhage of the Agar-Onida-Harrold parish to serve the District as Missionary-at-Large in the Black Hawk community. Pastor Redhage accepted the call and was installed on February 8, 1987. Articles of Incorporation and Bylaws were produced and received the approval of the District Board of Directors at its March 1987 meeting. This opened the way for its incorporation and reception as a congregation in the Lutheran Church – Missouri Synod.

Lord of Life Lutheran Church, Sioux Falls, South Dakota

In the early 1980's, discussions were held among the members of the Board of Directors of the South Dakota District about the possibility of a mission start in eastern Sioux Falls. Because the southeast section of Sioux Falls was experiencing the most growth and promised future growth as well, the Board of Directors purchased a 9.8 acre parcel of land adjacent to the intersection of 33rd Street and Sycamore Avenue with a grant from Forward In Remembrance.

As building of homes grew in this area, the Board targeted the calling of a mission developer for late 1986 or early 1987.

Several calls were issued until finally the Lord chose the Reverend Robert E. Heckmann of Decatur, Illinois to accept His call into this field. Pastor Heckmann was installed on April 10, 1988 at Christ Lutheran Church, Sioux Falls as Mission Developer to the southeast area of Sioux Falls.

Missionary Heckmann, together with members of other Sioux Falls congregations, began canvassing the area in order to discover people interested in becoming involved in a new mission.

The first planning meeting with interested families of the mission was held August 7, 1988. Bible studies were held weekly.

The first worship service was held on Sunday, September 25, 1988 at Sioux Falls Christian High School, 17th and Sycamore Avenue.

The need for a church facility soon became apparent. On July 14, 1996, ground was broken in the southeast area of Sioux Falls for Lord of Life Lutheran Church. The new structure was built by volunteer laborers as well as Synod's Laborers for Christ. The time for

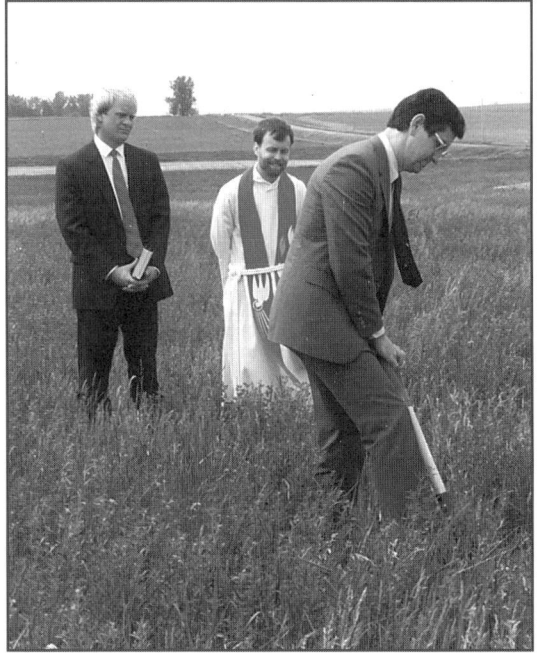

Groundbreaking at Lord of Life, Sioux Falls - June 11, 1989 Congregational Chairman Tim Vanderpann, Pastor Robert Heckmann, President Raymond Hartwig

rejoicing and dedication of the new building was set for February 16, 1997.

God's continued grace and blessings accompany this congregation as it grows dynamically in this part of our District.

Resurrection Lutheran Church, Sioux Falls, South Dakota

Members of Our Redeemer Lutheran Church of Sioux Falls suggested that a new mission be started in western Sioux Falls. This first meeting occurred on March 18, 1990 to discuss the possibility of a preaching station in this area. The enthusiasm showed the need to establish such a presence. On April 22, 1990 the first worship service (together with Sunday School) was held in the District Office building with the Reverend Howard Shane, Pastor of Our Redeemer leading the service. Early services were held in the District Office.

It soon became evident that a larger facility would become necessary to accommodate the increased attendance. On October 7, 1990 services were moved to the Oscar Howe Elementary School at 2801 Valley View Road. When attendance averaged 40 people, discussions began about the need to organize an independent congregation.

Resurrection Lutheran was received into membership of the Lutheran Church – Missouri Synod during the South Dakota District Convention on February 4, 1991. Candidate L. Scott Spiehs from Concordia Theological Seminary in Fort Wayne, IN accepted the congregation's call to serve as its first pastor, and was installed June 23, 1991.

Property was purchased by the South Dakota District LCMS on 26th Street and South Brookshire as the future site for Resurrection Lutheran. In March of 1992 the property was gifted to the mission congregation by the District.

A building committee was established and architectural services and construction personnel were hired to begin the first phase of the building. This first phase called for a 6,300 square foot sanctuary with seating for at least 250.

On May 3, 1992 a groundbreaking ceremony was held with Pastor Spiehs serving as liturgist and President Raymond Hartwig serving as officiant and preacher.

Thanksgiving Eve, November 25, 1992 was the date of the first worship held in the new worship facility with 100+ members and guests attending.

On January 1, 1993 this house of worship was dedicated to God's glory and honor and for the welfare of his people. The laying of the cornerstone was completed a few weeks later due to extreme cold weather at this time. Membership at the time of dedication and cornerstone-laying was 106 baptized souls with 87 communicant members.

In 1993, an additional 1,800 square feet was extended to the north side of the building. This addition was completed in February of 1994. In 1994 Sioux Falls Lutheran School, (of which Resurrection is a member) added a west-side pre-school which was housed at Resurrection.

Blessed Redeemer Lutheran Church, Brandon, South Dakota

On April 19, 1990 several families from Faith Lutheran Church in Sioux Falls, along with several families from other congregations of the LCMS in Sioux Falls, requested the Voters' Assembly of Faith Lutheran to "mother" a preaching station in Brandon. Seeing the great potential to spread the Gospel in this growing community, the voters of Faith granted the request and its pastor, Reverend Larry G. Borgelt led the first worship service on May 13, 1990 at the Brandon Junior High School.

This preaching station quickly developed into a congregation. The South Dakota District approved a constitution on December 2, 1990 and Blessed Redeemer was officially received as a member of the Lutheran Church – Missouri Synod on its Charter Sunday, December 30, 1990.

The need for a building had to be addressed. In February of 1991 the South Dakota District purchased a building site on the west side of Brandon. Groundbreaking took place on June 16, 1991 and the cornerstone was laid on Thanksgiving Day, November 28, 1991, during the first worship service held in the new building.

Because of the tremendous potential in Brandon and the growing need for pastoral services, Faith Lutheran called an Associate Pastor to help with this ministry. This would allow further needs at Faith to be met as well as continuing to serve the needs of this "daughter" congregation. Candidate Perry R. Bauer from Concordia Seminary in St. Louis, MO received and accepted the call. He was installed as Faith's Associate Pastor on July 14, 1991.

As the congregation grew, so also their needs grew. The need for a full-time pastor was felt and on June 14, 1992, Blessed Redeemer extended a call to Pastor Perry Bauer to serve them full-time. He accepted that call and was installed as Pastor on August 16, 1992.

Blessed Redeemer currently has a pre-school to serve the large number of children in the community of Brandon. They have also added an educational facility which houses Sunday School and other educational meetings as well as a large multi-purpose gymnasium for use by the growing congregation and community.

Holy Cross Lutheran Church, Dakota Dunes, South Dakota

As the community of Dakota Dunes took shape in the early 1990's the South Dakota District took an interest in establishing a mission in this area of South Dakota. So it was in December of 1993 that the District called the Reverend Glen Wurdeman as Missionary-at-Large to the southeastern South Dakota mission field. Its early beginnings were established at 952 North Sioux Point Road, when worship services were held in the basement. Bible classes and Vacation Bible School took place there as well.

The first worship service was held in September of 1994. The preschool began as a major focus of outreach for the congregation in September of 1995.

In November of 1995 a Charter Service was held and the congregation became incorporated and chose as its name, "Holy Cross Evangelical Lutheran Church of Southern Union County." In February of 1996 Pastor Wurdeman was installed as Pastor to the members of Holy Cross Lutheran congregation.

It was a happy time, when on May 1, 1997, land was purchased at the corner of Dakota Dunes Boulevard and Bison Trail for a permanent church facility. Groundbreaking was held at that time and construction began on the building in June of 1997, using Laborers for Christ as the general contractor. It was with great rejoicing that the first service was held in the new facility in December of 1997. The building was finished and landscaping completed in April of 1998.

Pastor Kevin Vogts was called to Holy Cross Lutheran Church in November of 2002 and installed as its pastor in February of 2003.

God's choice blessings have been abundant in the life of Holy Cross Lutheran Church and we pray that those blessings would continue into the future!

Peace Lutheran Church, Brookings, South Dakota

It was in September of 1995 that a number of people, especially members from Mount Calvary in Brookings met in homes for Bible Study, prayer, and song. They also began discussing the possibility of forming a new LCMS congregation in the city of Brookings.

So it was on October 29, 1995 that they met officially for Bible Study and Sunday School.

On March 25, 1996, the Board of Directors of the South Dakota District, LCMS accepted Peace congregation as a congregation of the Synod. On April 5, President Raymond Hartwig led the first service on Good Friday.

During April 1996 the congregation began the call process.

God chose the Reverend Timothy Rynearson of Wolsey and Wessington to accept the first call to be pastor at Peace Lutheran Church. Pastor Rynearson was installed November 17, 1996.

Vacation Bible School at Peace Lutheran, Brookings, SD July 2005

Because of the growth of the congregation, members began to look toward the start of a new building. A pre-school was opened in September of 1997 for the members of the congregation as well as the public. This pre-school has met with huge success in the community, helping to meet the needs of young families.

Peace opened a Day Care and Kindergarten in August of 1998. Mrs. Warren (Carol) Uecker was commissioned and installed as the first parochial school teacher at Peace Lutheran on August 30, 1998. On September 19, 1999 groundbreaking for a new building was held at 12th Street South. Peace today worships in that new facility and ministers to a large number of children entrusted to its care.

Rosebud Lutheran Mission, Rosebud, South Dakota

Over the years, many pastors and congregations have ministered to the Indian communities on the Rosebud Reservation. But in the mid 1990's, largely due to the efforts of Pastor Tom Zeller of Norris, serious efforts became the order of the day. Pastor Zeller, together with his members from St. John's Lutheran Church, gave out free ice-water and coffee at the Rosebud Fair, attracting many Indians who would then hear about the Savior, Jesus Christ. The question would then be asked if they would be interested in attending a Bible Class. Because the response was very positive, Pastor Zeller requested that the District consider calling someone to help in this ministry. The time he needed to devote to his congregations as well as the Indian Ministry left no time for doing the job that he knew needed to be done.

Reverend Andrew Utecht and his group at Rosebud

In 1996 the South Dakota District Board of Directors met and extended a call to Pastor Robert Utecht of Immanuel Lutheran Church in Dimock to be the first full-time District-called missionary to the Native Americans on the Rosebud Reservation. Pastor Utecht accepted that call and was installed at Immanuel Lutheran as Immanuel's missionary to the Native Americans on October 10, 1993 by President Raymond Hartwig. Now came the task of finding a parsonage for the Pastor and his wife as well as a place for worship. The tribe had given Pastor Zeller an old "trashed" double-wide trailer. Together with the members of Mount Calvary, Huron, this trailer was repaired and made usable and became the Rosebud Lutheran Mission worship facility.

The first worship service was held on November 21, 1993 at 10:00 a.m. Eight Indian people came, plus five members of Pastor Utecht's family. They sat on chairs loaned to them from St. John Lutheran Church of Norris. Since there was no organist at that time, the hymns were sung from the Lutheran Hymnal, copies of which were given by Immanuel of Dimock. Singing was done a capella. Pastor Utecht's first sermon was from Psalm 103:13 "Like as a Father pitieth His children, so the Lord pitieth them that fear Him." He tried to show how God is a loving Father who surrounds His people with His love and cares for them if they but trust Him. Bible study was held following worship services.

The Indian people asked for services again the following Sunday and inquired about the possibility of Sunday School for the children. This was done by Pastor Utecht's wife, Donna.

As the congregation grew, albeit slowly, better facilities were necessary. Today the Rosebud Lutheran Mission meets in a church which was purchased in the community and updated with help from members of various congregations in the District.

One of the very beneficial things held each year is Vacation Bible School. The opportunity to minister to larger numbers of children has become a reality through these VBS schools.

Another ministry which has met with large acceptance is the daily devotional radio broadcast with Pastor Utecht.

As Pastor Utecht began to talk about retirement, the District began looking for someone to replace him in this most important role as Pastor in this Indian community. God provided for this need in the person of Pastor and Mrs. Utecht's son, Andrew Utecht, a candidate from Concordia Seminary. Today Pastor Andrew Utecht, his wife Lori, and their children live on the reservation and serve the people there with the preaching of the Gospel of Jesus Christ. We pray God's rich blessings upon this special ministry of our District as it reaches ever more people with the Gospel of Jesus Christ.

Our Redeemer Lutheran Church, Rapid City, South Dakota

Our Redeemer Lutheran Church, North Rapid City, SD

Our Redeemer Lutheran Church held its first service on January 23, 1999 in the old United Way Building at 610 Kansas City Street. The congregation consisted of 35 members and was served by Pastor David Schwan and Mr. David Laudenschlager. Pastor Raymond H. Adams, present pastor, was installed on September 19, 1999.

In February of 2000 the congregation moved to 610 St. Francis Street, sharing a building with The Living Word Church. The current facility at 910 Wood Avenue was purchased in April of 2004 from the City of Rapid City. Members of the congregation did much of the remodeling to make the building what it is today. The first service was conducted there on May 23, 2004. The present sanctuary, a remodeled gymnasium, housed the first service on April 3, 2005.

Blessed Emmanuel Lutheran Church, Sturgis, South Dakota

Largely through the efforts of Pastor Gordon Goldammer and members of Grace Lutheran Church in Deadwood, South Dakota, the need was shown for a mission congregation in the Sturgis area. On September 14, 1998, Pastor Goldammer, Pastor Robert Utecht and Pastor Gene Bauman met with interested people and helped organize a congregation. Pastor Gordon Goldammer from Grace Lutheran in Deadwood was asked to serve the new group of people in their efforts in Sturgis.

Services were first held in the Kinkaid Funeral Chapel in Sturgis and on May 2, 1999 were transferred to the Bear Butte Elementary School. Incorporation papers were filed in Pierre on February 16, 2000.

Land was purchased and given to the congregation by the South Dakota District of the LCMS on June 5, 2000.

On Pentecost Sunday, June 11, 2000 the Reverend Vernon Schindler, District President preached and chartered the new congregation as a member of the Lutheran Church – Missouri Synod. Groundbreaking was held for a new worship facility on July 1, 2000.

On December 3, 2000 the first service was held in the fellowship hall with the first service held in the church sanctuary on January 14, 2001. Pastor Lew Koch of Mount Calvary, Huron was called to be the first pastor and was installed on September 23, 2001. Reverend Robert Bailey then served as a vacancy pastor.

We pray God's rich blessings on Blessed Emmanuel Lutheran Church and its efforts to minister to the people of the Sturgis community and be-yond.

Risen Savior Lutheran Church, Tea, South Dakota

For some time the Board of Directors had been looking at the Harrisburg and Tea areas as the possible start of a new mission congregation. Both of these communities were having much growth due to the increased number of people who worked in Sioux Falls but wanted to live in a small nearby com-munity.

And so it was on October 28, 2002 that the Board of Directors, meeting via conference call, agreed to purchase 8.6 acres of land in Tea at the cost of $30,000 per acre.

In the summer of 2003, Howard Koosman, former District Executive Secretary and Lutheran Teacher/Principal was asked to gather some people together for Bible Study to form the nucleus of a mission group in the Tea community. This was started in February of 2003. The group met monthly in various homes and studied Paul's letters to the Christians in Corinth.

As the group continued to grow under God's blessings, the need became evident that worship services be held in the community for this group of Christians. March 7, 2004 over 50 people gathered at the Tea Area School District's primary gym for worship services and Sunday School. Pastor Rob-ert Moeller of Trinity Lutheran Church in Hartford agreed to serve the new mission group as interim pastor.

Because of the young families living in Tea and the number of young children, the need was strongly felt for a Lutheran pre-school in the commu-nity. The community was surveyed, showing that people were interested in such a venture. Mrs. Jim (Tracie) Phelps, a member of the mission group, was contracted to teach the pre-school together with Mrs. Vern (Belva) Schindler and Mrs. Robert (Aimee) Moeller assisting. In the fall of 2004, a Lutheran Pre-school was started in a house which was purchased by the District and repaired and cleaned up by members of the congregation. This house at 505 North Carla serves also as a place for congregational meetings, offices, etc.

Our District's newest mission, Risen Savior, Tea, SD - Charter Sunday, December 2004

On December 13, 2004 the congregation's Articles of Incorporation were approved by the District Board of Directors. The name of Risen Savior Lutheran Church was chosen by the mission group for the new congregation. The first baptism was held on May 16 when Pastor Moeller baptized Bradley Grave.

The congregation now worships in the new Tea area Middle School/High School commons. Pastor Christopher M. Boehnke serves as the first full-time resident Pastor.

Chapter 13
Former Ministries of The South
Dakota District

New Underwood, South Dakota

As there is no written record, the early information about this preaching station is drawn from the recollection of others. It was about 1910 that New Underwood was visited by a Lutheran pastor for the first time. This was Pastor Amen who lived in Hereford. The Synodical Report from the South Dakota District (1910) mentions that he had 18 worshippers. After he had served New Underwood for more than a year, he accepted another call; and during the vacancy, representatives from the Iowa Synod worked in the region. Three different pastors of the Iowa Synod served this area for approximately five years. Very soon after his arrival, the people did not like the last of the three and would not accept him any longer. It was almost four years before Pastor Nitschke received a call to serve these people, while at the same time he served the people in Rapid City. "I have been here since September. The present statistics for this preaching station stands at : families – 10; souls – 48; in Confirmation Instruction – 5; average worship attendance – around 25; Sunday School – 10.

"Since January, we have been hoping to form a congregation. As soon as possible, when we can have a proper meeting of the members, we will organize a congregation here. There is no church building available here in New Underwood. During the year the Catholic Church may be available for us to acquire, as they will build a new church; and we have already received a price for their building. At the moment we use a small school house, which is very inconvenient since it is meant to be used by small children.

"A parsonage is to be desired. Believe me as you draw a picture of our living conditions here. We live in four back rooms over the hardware store. Each room measures about 10 feet x 10 feet and the two back rooms in the winter can not be heated all the time (Northwest winds blow the smoke into the room so that I must often move my study into the kitchen. But worse than that is the inconvenience we find ourselves in. The store below is a gathering place for the local people. So many times one hears the most terrible sounds, not in a musical sense, but in a moral sense. The coarse language of the male inhabitants fills the shop with their cursing every possible object in every sentence. One such inconvenience occurs when it disrupts the Confirmation instruction – which many times must be held

in the kitchen. I hope, that if possible, during the coming year a residence might be built, or at least a more suitable room be gotten."

Farmingdale, South Dakota

"Farmingdale was first visited by Pastor Kieszling. He preached there twice in 1910. Pastor O. Heilmann soon followed him. The preaching station, at that time, numbered 19 souls according to the 1910 statistical Yearbook. Since 1913 Pastor Nitschke has been serving these people from Rapid City. Here too, there is no church property available. The worship services are held in a house. At the moment, this preaching station numbers 8 families and 44 souls. They come together from a large area and worship services are not very regular."

Creston, South Dakota

"Creston is also a part of Pastor Heilmann's district. In 1910 there were 32 souls there. The place is only now getting started. There are only two families there; but this fall I preached there. The one family still goes to Farmingdale, while the other attends at Scenic."

Scenic, South Dakota

"This place, too, was first served by Pastor Heilmann. In 1910 Scenic numbered 14 souls. After Pastor Heilmann served them, Pastor Nitschke came to this place also. Scenic numbers about 10 families at present. I write deliberately "about." Scenic is a mixed group. There are many mixed marriages there and the Congregationalists find that there is considerable confusion over the construction of their church building, as it was intended to be a community church. The future of this place is very uncertain. I am convinced that there are at least a few true Lutherans who wish to remain Lutheran. We make use of the new Congregational Church for our worship services. Worship services here are still very irregular, as in Farmingdale, where the people live in a widely scattered area."

Additional Information About This Area

"North of Underwood, in the area of Haydraw and Hereford, there should be two settlements where you will find Lutherans; and as soon as spring comes, I will explore this area. Also to the east of Underwood, in the area around Owanka and Wasta there are a few Lutheran families; and I already have received information that in the northern part of the area, there are people there that I need to visit, but I know very little about this eastern part of the region. That is as much as I know. I will as soon as possible visit these places. In the fall I had enough to do in visiting the old places and becoming acquainted with the people there."

(Translated by Reverend Vernon L. Schindler, May 2005)

Trinity Lutheran Church, Dixon, South Dakota

Because of the very scant records on file in the District Archives, the following information is all that we have to publish about Trinity Lutheran Church, now disbanded, of Dixon, South Dakota.

Our records indicated that Trinity Lutheran Church was organized in 1909. Records do not indicate whether they were a single congregation parish or whether they were linked with St. John of Gregory from the start. Sometime during its history, Trinity formed a dual parish with St. John of Gregory, South Dakota and was served by the same pastor.

Records also indicate that St. John of Gregory withdrew the parish alignment agreement in 1982, at which time Trinity was unable to support a pastor on its own and worship services ceased. There were various efforts made to continue worship services. However, because of low attendance, etc., records indicate that in 1984 the congregation was officially removed as a congregation of the Lutheran Church – Missouri Synod.

Zion Lutheran Church, Rockham, South Dakota

Records in the District Office are almost nothing on Zion Lutheran Church at Rockham, South Dakota. This congregation has been served by the pastor who also served Redfield and Doland at one time. However because of declining membership Zion was closed on December 8, 1974 with the members going to Messiah Lutheran in Redfield or to the ALC church in Miller, South Dakota.

Gethsemane Lutheran Church, Mobridge, South Dakota

It was in 1964 that the first service was held at Gethsemane Lutheran Church in Mobridge. The church edifice was dedicated on January 26, 1964. Pastor Robert Utecht of Gettysburg served the congregation as interim pastor until May 31, 1964 when the Reverend Edwin Schlade was installed as the first regular pastor of this congregation. Following Pastor Schlade's ministry to the people at Gethsemane Lutheran was the Reverend Philip Mueller of Huron who accepted the call and was installed on January 7, 1968.

Because the South Dakota District LCMS believed that the numbers were not adequate to make the financial investment, the District Convention voted to close Gethsemane Lutheran. At the time of closing, the congregation numbered 50 souls, 30 which were communicant members.

Only eternity will tell the number of souls that were touched by the Gospel message during this short time that Gethsemane Lutheran was in operation.

Zion Lutheran Church, Kadoka, South Dakota

Even though many of our Lutheran people in South Dakota are unaware that we have ever had a Lutheran church at Kadoka, it is true that early services and preliminary work was begun among the German Lutherans near Kadoka in the spring of 1907 under the leadership of the Reverend Gade of White Lake, SD. Following Pastor Gade was Reverend Theodore Kissling, who was ordained and installed at St. Peter Lutheran Church of Midland and helped in organizing the Zion Lutheran congregation at Kadoka. This happened at a meeting on July 30, 1907. The congregation at that meeting also resolved to join the Lutheran Church – Missouri Synod. Its name in the beginning was "The Evangelical Lutheran Zion's Congregation of Kadoka, Stanley County, South Dakota." At a congregation meeting on October 23, 1910 it was decided to form a committee which would look for a proper location for a church cemetery. It was decided in January of 1911 that land would be purchased at the F.P. Werner farm for this cemetery. (Ancestors of Pastor John Werner of Clayton, SD.) In 1926 the congregation decided to alternate between German and English preaching for its worship services. In 1933 the congregation decided after some discussion to have two English services and one German service per month. In 1927 the congregation went to the envelope system for financial giving to the work of the Lord and His Church.

In 1938 a bid of $135 was put on a school building to be used as a house of worship. This building served as a church and was dedicated in September 1938 by Pastor Theodore Wieting. Up until this time services were held in private homes or rented school buildings. For a short time in 1945, a building was purchased in Kadoka, but sold a year later. An acre of ground was purchased from Mr. Grabel for a church site where the final church was located.

The congregation then in 1946 applied for a loan of $2,500 from the Church Extension Fund to purchase the church building from Peace congregation south of Stamford for $1,000. This building was then moved to Kadoka on January 14, 1948. After some repair and remodeling, the church was dedicated in July of 1948 by Pastor Theodore Wieting, the same pastor who had dedicated the first church ten years earlier. The church building in the country was then sold in 1949 for $450. With these monies, the congregation bought new pews for its present church.

The pastor at this time resided at the parsonage at St. Peter Lutheran Church near Midland. The Kadoka congregation had been served all its years as a joint venture with St. Peter of Midland (except 1925 and 1926 when Pastor Philip Mueller, former pastor and District President of our District, served Zion of Kadoka).

When you travel east from Kadoka you can still see the cemetery as you look off to the North from the Interstate. Here lie the bodies of some of the faithful people who served their God in such wonderful ways at this congregation.

Zion Lutheran Church of Kadoka was closed in 1967, at which time it merged with the ALC in the town of Kadoka.

St. Paul Lutheran Church, Dallas, South Dakota: 1907-1950

Zion Lutheran Church, South Dallas, South Dakota: 1905-1950

West Carlock, South Dakota

Other Ministries Serving In Our District

Human Services Center, Yankton, South Dakota

For many years Pastor George Baumgartner served as Chaplain and Patient Advocate at the Human Services Center in Yankton. This ministry ended some years ago when Pastor Baumgartner retired.

Reverend George Baumgartner, Former Chaplain at Human Services Center in Yankton, SD

Sioux Falls Hospital Chaplaincy Program

One of the very valuable ministries of our District is that of Hospital Chaplain to the Sioux Falls Hospitals. Pastor O.D. Brack has served our District in this position for many years. Pastor Brack is willing to call on any member of one of the congregations of our District if someone lets him know of a need.

Chaplain O.D. Brack ministers to a patient in a Sioux Falls hospital, October 2005.

Campus Ministry

A number of congregations serve the young people attending our State and other universities in South Dakota. We thank God for the willingness of these congregations to serve the young people in this critical time of their life.

LWML

The Lutheran Women's Missionary League is a vital organization in our District in which the women of the LWML reach out with their mites and talents to bring the Gospel of Jesus Christ to the world. They financially support many projects in our District that need assistance.

Host Committee for the 23rd biennial convention of the international LWML. The convention was held June 26-29, 1989 at the Rushmore Plaza Civic Center, Rapid City, SD with the theme "Seek His Face Always" based on 1 Chronicles 16:11.

LLL

Lutheran Hour Ministries has also served our District for many years. They also reach out with the Gospel in many ways, among which is "The Lutheran Hour – Bringing Christ to the Nations" heard each Sunday on radio.

Main Street Living

Main Street Living is a weekly television broadcast which uses programs from "This is the Life" as well as one of our District pastors who has a brief message and worship service in connection with each weekly program. This has been a very valuable ministry to many of the shut-in members of our congregations.

Ethiopian Ministry

Faith, Sioux Falls, began work with Ethiopian Lutherans in May 2005. This Ethiopian group, numbering about twenty, conducts its own services in the Oromic language, in Faith's Shepherd Room. At times, the Faith congregation joins in worship and other activities with its Ethiopian brothers and sisters in Christ.

Ethiopian ministry at Faith Lutheran Church, Sioux Falls, SD 2005

Pine Ridge Native American Ministry

Although Reverend Robert Utecht retired from his work on the Rosebud Reservation, he and his wife Donna continue their work among the Native Americans at the Pine Ridge Reservation.

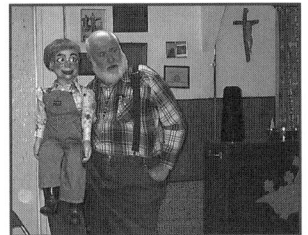

Reverend Robert Utecht shares his "Puppet Ministry" with those at Pine Ridge.

Sudanese Ministry

Zion, Sioux Falls, works with Sudanese immigrants.

Sudanese Ministry

Youth Ministry

The youth of the District stay active with various events. An annual gathering is held for the older youth and an annual camp for the younger ones.

Working on the LFL crosses during a District Youth Gathering in Spearfish

Inspector (Reverend) Scott Sailer inspects the cabins at Camp Minneboji.

District Presidents
and Their Terms of Office

Reverend A.F. Breihan
1906-1912

Reverend J.D. Ehlen
1912-1918

Reverend E.J. Jehn
1918-1921

Reverend F.W. Leyhe
1921-1936

Reverend Walter Nitschke
1936-1951

Reverend Philip H. Mueller
1951-1961

Reverend E.O. Luessenhop
1961-1968

Reverend Leonard A. Eberhard
1968-1970

Reverend Arthur J. Crosmer
1970-1978

Rev. Dr. Paul G. Wendling
1978-1988

Rev. Dr. Raymond L. Hartwig
1988-1998

Rev. Dr. Vernon L. Schindler
1998-Present

District Office Buildings

2009 South Sherman Avenue in Sioux Falls was Executive Secretary Nieting's home and also the first location for the District Office in 1956.

2116 South Minnesota Avenue was the second home to the SD District Office in the 1960's.

101 East 38th Street was the third location for the District Office in the early 1970's.

3501 Gateway Boulevard is the present home of the SD District Office. This building was possible due to a generous gift to the District specifically for this purpose. We welcome visitors anytime.

Congregational Index